THE
HIDDEN
ORACLE
of INDIA

THE MYSTERY OF INDIA'S
NAADI PALM READERS

First published by O Books, 2008
O Books is an imprint of John Hunt Publishing
Ltd., The Bothy, Deershot Lodge, Park Lane,
Ropley, Hants, SO24 0BE, UK
office1@o-books.net
www.o-books.net

Distribution in:

UK and Europe
Orca Book Services
orders@orcabookservices.co.uk
Tel: 01202 665432 Fax: 01202 666219 Int. code
(44)

USA and Canada
NBN
custserv@nbnbooks.com
Tel: 1 800 462 6420 Fax: 1 800 338 4550

Australia and New Zealand
Brumby Books
sales@brumbybooks.com.au
Tel: 61 3 9761 5535 Fax: 61 3 9761 7095

Far East (offices in Singapore, Thailand, Hong
Kong, Taiwan)
Pansing Distribution Pte Ltd
kemal@pansing.com
Tel: 65 6319 9939 Fax: 65 6462 5761

South Africa
Alternative Books
altbook@peterhyde.co.za
Tel: 021 447 5300 Fax: 021 447 1430

Text copyright Andrew and Angela Donovan 2008

Design: Stuart Davies

ISBN: 978 1 84694 074 3

A CIP catalogue record for this book is available
from the British Library.

Printed in the US by Maple Vail

O Books operates a distinctive and ethical publishing philosophy in
all areas of its business, from its global network of authors to
production and worldwide distribution.

No trees were cut down to print this particular book. The paper is
100% recycled, with 50% of that being post-consumer. It's processed
chlorine-free, and has no fibre from ancient or endangered forests.

This production method on this print run saved approximately
thirteen trees, 4,000 gallons of water, 600 pounds of solid waste,
990 pounds of greenhouse gases and 8 million BTU of energy. On its
publication a tree was planted in a new forest that O Books is
sponsoring at The Village www.thefourgates.com

THE
HIDDEN
ORACLE
of INDIA

THE MYSTERY OF INDIA'S
NAADI PALM READERS

ANDREW AND ANGELA DONOVAN

BOOKS

Winchester, UK
Washington, USA

CONTENTS

Dedicated to Swami Premananda

ACKNOWLEDGEMENTS

Both Andrew and I are deeply grateful to Elias Kasmi, our most gracious host in India, for the endless hours, days and weeks he tirelessly spent acting as the 'Mr Fixer' for all our needs – and especially for being such an efficient translator throughout each one of our Naadi sessions. We thank him as a dear and close friend, without whom this journey would not have been destined at the time it was! Through his efforts may all his puja be cleared and his own personal leaf finally now be found.

We give thanks too to our close friends Kate Townsend and Sheena MacBrayne, who have bravely shared their own truths on the Naadis in this book. Thank you both so much.

And we give great blessings to the Naadi holy-men in Delhi for their calm, patience and tolerance whilst we struggled so persistently on too numerous occasions to find the palm-leaves of our friends. Bless them for assisting us on our journey of learning, and for accepting with such good grace the fact that we would be alerting so many more to visit them from that moment on.

Yet we cannot forget how it all started, so, lastly, we give heartfelt thanks to our great tv friend and facilitator Lesley Davies, who kick-started the whole affair on a whim of divine synchronicity, so realizing the 'Deal or No Deal' of our lives....

FOREWORD

As a great friend of Angela and Andrew, the authors of this book, I have found it a great comfort to know that I am not alone in my search for the meaning of my very existence in this troubled world.

The search for peace of mind and tranquility in the shifting sands of our everyday lives can only be found within ourselves. What we call our conscience is in fact a higher self with a perfect morality that does not judge our actions but, because of its existence, something causes us to judge ourselves. If we do, and are not pleased with something we have done, it is a good sign – we are not lost.

Many people I know do feel lost, and wonder what their life here on earth is for. Does it have any meaning? The thing most of these people forget is that happiness and the contentment of just being lies within themselves and not with the acquisition of more material objects; to have sincere and understanding friends lasts far longer than a new car or the latest fashion.

My advice is to relax and listen to your inner voice. Yes, you do have one, you hear it every day, and if you believe this as I always have, talk back to it and ask for peace of mind and guidance not to plan ahead – Fate and Destiny might have something quite different planned for you, for your life has already been pre-determined.

Read this book and hopefully you will have some understanding. If you don't, it won't make any difference, for your future is already written. But don't be surprised if it is more – or sometimes less – than you expect.

Jeremy Lloyd

INTRODUCTION

'Love nothing but that which comes to you
woven in the pattern of your destiny......'
Marcus Aurelius (121-80)

They say you cannot rewrite history. But you can add to it, filling in some of its gaping holes with truths when you find them. When we first stumbled upon the story of the Naadi palm leaf readers of India, we were not trying to solve any great mystery. We were simply visiting India to attend a wedding, excited to experience the great beauty of that land for the first time. But what we found there changed our lives forever.

The word *'Naadi'* has at least seven different meanings. In the Tamil language *'Naadi'* means *'in pursuit of'* or *'in search of...'* *'Naadi'* also means *'those who are destined to come on their own accord'*.

Now, after several years of research, travel and inquiry, we are able to say with confidence that the story we present in the pages that follow fills one of the great historical gaps yet to be resolved, one which concerns free will, our own humanity and the course of our civilization.

When you come across something entirely fresh and new in your life – of the wholly 'unknown' variety – it will either interest you enough for you to want to know a very great deal more about it, or it will pass you by almost unnoticed, not resonating sufficiently at the time. You're too busy, too stressed or you have too much else on your plate to think about an even bigger picture, so you let it pass.

But in this instance we found there was another way too. The mystery of the Naadis came right out of left field, like a flash flood. It hit, created havoc, and afterwards nothing was ever the same again. Suddenly we found ourselves asking big questions. Is it possible to find out who we truly are, to learn the details of our whole life's journey, in advance? Could it be that the struggles and difficulties that we face are a direct result of our actions in a previous life? Is it possible that we were destined to seek answers to these questions at the exact time and date that we do? Finally, is it possible for all of these specific revelations about our lives to be covered on palm leaves written 3,000 years before we were born?

The answer we now believe is yes – for we have seen and heard it with our own eyes. What was intended as a short and simple side-trip taking only an hour of our time was the start of an intensely spiritual journey, and became a demanding, frustrating historical research project with ramifications way beyond our expectations.

We were affected very differently by this journey. While one of us (Angela) initially found the whole experience greatly uplifting – to the extent of receiving confirmation concerning her life's journey – it was not the same for the other (Andrew), who suffered the severest of shocks as his lifelong 'dis-belief' system was shattered completely in less than a single afternoon.

A few months later, having had time to digest the experience, we both found ourselves excited and greatly intrigued by what we had so unexpectedly come across through sheer synchronicity. We just had to get out there and solve the mystery for ourselves as best we could.

In the pages that follow we try to set down, openly and honestly, the facts behind the mystery of the Naadi palm leaves just as we found them. We base our findings not only on our own experiences but on those of a handful of others who have also visited the Naadis. Two have been willing to share their experiences of what took place and how it led them to make great shifts in their own lives. Each of us has a story to tell, with differing personal reactions and conclusions, and neither is commonplace or ordinary. For what people discover upon hearing the Naadis is far too personal, powerful and intimate for that.

* * *

India is a sleeping giant with a seemingly eternal way of life. She is a country of contradictions, rushing to take her place in the 21st century yet not forgetting her storied past. In her busy-ness there is stillness too. The cities are hectic, teeming with people, hooting traffic, decrepit overloaded buses and tik-tik taxis powered by natural gas – everything is a rainbow of color, smell and a cacophony of noise. To westerners like us it was a complete culture shock, venturing there for the first time. Cows wander across busy main roads as if they owned them – which they do – or sit chewing the cud in the central reservations between lanes of roaring traffic, while hordes of curious, opportunistic monkeys commandeer the quieter Delhi roads in the early mornings. But the hustle and bustle is only a sensory shock. If one sits in a calm space for a period of time it is possible to feel the intensity of 'being' that exists amongst the population. There is a wonderful blend of acceptance and affirmation, a peaceful yet dynamic sense of 'now' that has been all but lost in the consumer-led credit-bound western world. And away from the cities there is peace and tranquility in abundance. The much slower pace of agrarian life allows for simple, uncomplicated pleasures. The people continue to respect the profound and lasting philosophy of the ancient Seers and the innumerable, magnificent temples that serve them.

It is perhaps only in such a contradictory setting that the Naadi palm leaf readers can thrive while somehow remaining almost unknown to most of India's general population and the outside world ... and at the same time reveal, with utter conviction, secret words first transcribed three millennia ago onto ancient palm leaves that have patiently awaited their rendezvous with those they speak of centuries later. In our case this was in a third-floor room in a busy back street suburb of New Delhi... a well-hidden oracle, whose time it now is to come to light.

The tradition of the Naadi readers is as ancient as it is obscure. It is said that between three and five thousand years ago Lord Shiva accessed the 'Akashic records' – a term used by the ancient Hindus to mean the records that exist holding all information on the past, present and future of the entire Universe – which he did in order to document the lives of every being that had lived, who lives now and would ever live on Earth.

He then relayed them to his seven chosen Seers, or disciples, for their physical inscription onto palm leaves.

These leaves – 'case histories' for want of a better phrase – were woven into bundles and stored in ancient royal libraries until they would be called for and individually identified by those aware of this knowledge and seeking the true purpose of their lives – something that can seemingly only be done at the time appointed by each leaf to do so, no sooner and no later.

We write more on all of this later; suffice it to say here that we can only thank the stillness of India for keeping her secrets all this time and for providing a safe haven for the fragile, dusty leaves on which the hidden truths of our lives were written.

* * *

So what is happening in the world today that requires us to know such truths? What is new that needs airing? Can strange writings on antiquated palm leaves really make a difference to the world we live in today?

For us it has, so our quest here is to share our experiences of the 'oracle' we discovered with people who wish to know more about it. Although it is becoming more and more obvious that the world today is heading for some major upheavals, we have come to believe we will all be better prepared to deal with whatever takes place in the coming years if we know our destined role within it. Such 'true knowing', under-standing the destiny that has been written for us, can surely help to remove the fears and anxieties that otherwise could overcome us and rule.

To some skeptics, our conclusions about the mystery of the Naadi palm leaves will be incomprehensible or unacceptable, taking it all just a step too far. To others it may well be a truth they have been waiting to hear. We can only suggest that having read this book you decide for yourself. Those whose destiny is written may very well follow the same journey we did, to cross the oceans and enter the world of the Naadis to seek and find their individual leaf. If our experience is anything to go by, those that do so will never be the same again. Their leaf will be waiting for them if the time appointed is right.

In essence there are only two questions you now need to ask. The first is:

"Is it possible that this life I'm living was chosen by me, and for me, thousands of years ago?"

And the second:

"Am I ready to know my truth, and the truth of the world, in advance of time?"

If either or both of these questions interests or intrigues you, then you won't be disappointed. It's an astounding adventure. Everything you want to know is out there waiting for you, and will be available to you when you are ready to receive it.

CHAPTER ONE

A Journey Into the Unknown – How We Found the Naadi
Palm Readers
Angela:

Andrew and I had been asked to do a short film for *Animal Planet* and had decided to shoot a section of the footage at our home in the countryside and film it over a weekend. To help get it right, a top UK producer whom we know well thought to involve a close professional colleague called Elias, an Indian film director whom she had previously worked with, who was visiting from Mumbai at the time. Immediately we got on very well with him and over the weekend we became ever firmer and closer friends, so that by the time Sunday evening came round, it was as if we had known him forever – a true delight, especially when such pleasant surprises happen so unexpectedly.

It was through that very first encounter that our long relationship with Elias began. Months later when we (unexpectedly) received an invitation to his sister's wedding in Kashmir, we felt very flattered, pleased and excited. It was a wonderful opportunity, one that we knew we couldn't miss, for here was a chance to experience a very intimate moment in Indian family life, one not usually offered to 'outsiders', let alone westerners. It was also a chance to see India for the very first time and in particular the wonderfully romantic setting of Kashmir, scene of beautiful house-boats on sparkling lakes, ancient Buddhist monasteries, dramatic landscapes, tumbling rivers, thick forests, emerald green rice fields and gentle waterways all making up the lush rolling countryside that had so reminded the Victorian colonials of dear old England and home.

Two days before we were due to fly out to Delhi, a friend phoned from Los Angeles and said, "You can't possibly go to India without seeing the palm-leaf readers". We had no idea what she was talking about. She enthusiastically told us that her close friend worked with Deepak Chopra and that he had had the most life-changing experience earlier in the year, with a group of Hindu holy men in south-eastern India who apparently gave amazing life readings based on nothing more than marks on your thumb. Once your individual thumbprint was categorized and located in the ancient archives, written on palm-leaves, we were told they could then give you an extremely detailed and accurate reading about your past, present and future lives – all from words written eons ago in ancient Sanskrit and etched onto a dusty palm-leaf.

To Andrew such a notion was utterly preposterous: "How could anyone possibly do that? It beggars belief... you're mad!" he protested. But to me it sounded like a most fascinating technique and certainly worth further investigation. After all, if Deepak Chopra thought they merited a visit, so could we!

So the friend quickly put the organizers in touch with us and they offered us help and advice regarding a way to meet these holy men while we were in India.

With the short time available to us for our whole trip, our first thoughts were to fly back to Delhi from the wedding a day or two early, fly down south to meet the holy men and have our readings, then fly back again to Delhi before immediately returning home to the UK. It seemed there was no other way – journeys by road or rail to the south would take far too long. Yet even by aeroplane it was already sounding an exhaustive marathon, and in hindsight and given more time to plan, we would have organized the whole affair over two to three weeks rather than the nine days that we had given ourselves.

But before making any other arrangements we decided to inform our host of the likely detour, given that we were expected to spend several days 'en famille' on the Dal Lake once the wedding ceremony was over. This was a signal honor for us and not one to be dismissed lightly as it would obviously appear very churlish or rude to leave even a minute early, however valid or intriguing the reason. So we gently tested the water with Elias first.

We needn't have worried. Serendipity was already with us. When we broached the idea with him on the phone he, being the true gentleman he is, put us at ease immediately and went on to say that he knew all about the palm-leaf readers as he had already tried to have a reading from them himself, albeit unsuccessfully. He also told us they had opened a center in Delhi so we now had no need to fly anywhere else. Accordingly, after gently warning us that we might not be 'found' either, he offered to arrange an appointment for us to visit them before flying to Kashmir: we had two hours to spare before check-in so they could at least take our thumbprints for categorizing whilst we were away. Honor and politeness saved, we readily agreed.

We arrived at Delhi Airport very late on a hot sweaty night to a deluge of warm monsoon rains, apparently the last of the season. "Welcome to India!" we thought, smiling through our sticky wet tiredness as we ploughed through Arrivals. Once past Immigration we found a very smart, uniformed driver waiting to meet us (thank goodness) and eagerly followed him through hundreds of people milling around as he pushed our heavily laden trolley out of the terminal and into the torrent of rain as though nothing at all was wrong. He was drenched in a flash but stolidly walked on in ankle deep floodwater to get to the hotel car.

As we followed, with our western clothes by now dripping wet and stuck to our bodies, one of our bags took a dive off the trolley and was submerged; nothing got said – it was all par for the course by then. The drive to the hotel was a real eye-opener. Due to the heaviness of the monsoon rains it took a long time to get there, with detours off roads that had by now completely disappeared under water or been blockaded off by police. This meant edging slowly around cars and buses left stranded in deserted rivers that had once been streets. No one but us seemed surprised by any of this, as we sat there trying to imagine how well London or New York would cope if they had such extremes of weather daily for several months each year.

The next morning Elias' driver was waiting for us at 9am. Not a word of English in him but delightful body language including bows, smiles and hand signals, so we could only repeat or agree with whatever he did in the hope that he knew what he was doing. An hour's drive took us through the – now dry – hectic main roads of Delhi and off into ever smaller and busier streets until we finally came into a thriving market area with all manner of shops, stalls and apartments jostling cheek-by-jowl amongst a network of narrow roads and even more cramped back-alleys. Halfway down one of these, he stopped the car, ushered us out, mumbled something and pointed to a gated doorway on one side with steep steps leading upwards. We followed his lead – up three flights – to arrive at a balcony overlooking the road on one side and an open entrance door on the other, by the side of which was a rickety ancient air-conditioning unit rattling away. Scores of shoes and socks littered the dusty balcony floor and a picture of a smiling God (Lord Shiva himself) sat over the door, decked about with a bright orange garland. The driver smiled, pointed us indoors then quickly left to return to the car. We were where we wanted to be, it seemed.

The custom is to take your shoes off at the door, bare feet only. Forget dirt, infections or diseases! Sheepishly we entered into the darkness. As our eyes adjusted we could see it was the reception area, a largish room full of white plastic chairs, with a long tatty desk at the far end covered in books and papers, and a glass-fronted bookcase behind, its yellowing documents locked away and clearly untouched for years. An old phone sat on the desk. Posters and newspaper cuttings adorned the walls, mostly of great age, but all the headlines were testifying to the wonders the Naadis have revealed for those who had seen them. Several Indians sat waiting, reading, talking quietly or playing with their mobile phones. Everyone looked up as we entered, surprise in their eyes, then smiled at us in wonder. The chatter stopped. Clearly westerners are uncommon here. We smiled back, embarrassed.

From behind the desk a short middle-aged man dressed in white stood up and looked at us inquiringly. He too was taken aback by our white faces and English clothes, but he said nothing, an uncertain smile on his lips. He bowed politely and waited, expectant. There was a long pause. Haltingly we tried to explain about our appointment, and suddenly he started work. Nothing was said that we could understand, as a huge book like a great ledger was dragged across the desk and opened up.

The white-robed man pointed at it meaningfully. We could see the book was full of fingerprints and crammed with page after page of single names and large, small, feint, fat, blotchy, dark, light, clear or smeared prints with dates, names and phone numbers written alongside them. It was a very thick book with dog-eared edges and a badly abused cover. The front of this book was marked '2004'; several other thick ledgers lying further away were dating back to 2001.

These people are clearly very busy. Idly we tried to think of the histories and dreams that each of these worn books must hold, each set of prints marking the start of a journey like ours.

Suddenly he stabbed the open page and gestured for us to put our thumbs on an ink-pad and plant them in the next available space. There was a moment of confusion as another man in jeans appeared from behind and tried to explain 'female left thumb' and 'male right thumb' using pidgin English and sign language, grinning at us all the while.

He explained that three prints are required for each of us, we presume for clarity. By each of our three prints we were to put our first names, whether we are male or female, the day's date and a phone number where to contact us – this last requirement was a tad difficult when we were traveling and unsure where we would be when they called, so we motioned that we would have someone ring them instead.

Watched closely by everyone in the room and with a great deal of amused background chatter, we laboriously dabbed our thumbs and placed our prints in the book, then entered our first names and dated them. The two men checked each set closely, nodded and stood up, smiling broadly. They shrugged and grinned – it seemed nothing more was required. Then, putting their hands together as if in prayer, they bowed and gestured us goodbye, telling us to ring them in a few days to find out more.

Realizing that was it, we did the same back to them and quietly left, put our shoes back on and headed for the airport.

Moving from Delhi to Kashmir is rather like traveling from Toronto to Mexico – a whole different ball game! The stringent, unsmiling security checks beat the US and UK for strictness any day of the week, but we had to remember that the Indians have had many years of militant insurgency both inside and outside Kashmir, so there is comfort to be had in the thorough, repeated checks that the immaculately-dressed personnel from the Indian Army carry out on you and all of your baggage as you make your slow way airside. Even if it is all done rather bluntly and unsmilingly.

* * *

It was a very grand Muslim wedding held at the old Maharajah's Palace outside Jammu. This is a truly amazing site in itself, with far-reaching views over the surrounding low plains and the rising, wooded regions behind them of southern Kashmir. Amongst the thousand guests we stood out like sore thumbs, and were privileged to note that we were the only westerners there – an honoring and very flattering experience. While we knew no one, everyone instantly knew of us, especially when they realized I was a spiritual medium!

The whole affair was truly splendid, an Indian equivalent of a Buckingham Palace tea party with everyone – men, women and children – all somehow related to the bride or groom's families; brothers, aunts, uncles, first-, second-, third-cousins to the umpteenth degree – all strutting around, talking and mingling, chatting and laughing and having fun amongst the thick swarms of flies, moths and sticky bugs drawn by the floodlights as the ceremony and the evening wore on.

The catering was a logistical and culinary triumph – a lavish feast of a seemingly endless series of courses, arranged across the well-kept wide-sweeping lawns in notionally separate zones for the hundreds of different Sikh, Hindu and Muslims present. The lively, noisy throng was a riot of vibrant, brilliant colors in wonderful dazzling saris, beautiful ceremonial dresses, sharp smart suits, stunning regalia, dapper braided uniforms, striking headgear and fabulous fine clothes, all melded together in an explosion of equally exotic sounds – the banging of drums, jingling of brass, trumpeting, wailing, beating, crying, laughing, singing, chattering and shouting that accompanied the wedding chants and women's songs as the ceremony progressed and processed slowly but surely to its completion in accordance with time-honored traditions. At one point there was even a corps of tartan-clad bagpipers strutting manfully around the place, puffing and blowing away, all very erect, resplendent and proud, with tall white plumes in their hats and eye-catching golden braid all over their uniformed big chests.

I was politely asked if I would meet and numerous local dignitaries and sit with them to offer my spiritual visions on their futures in business, wealth, health and happiness. I seem to have spent my life doing charity events from an early age, so it felt like a natural part of the occasion for me and I was delighted to offer what inspiration I could to all who asked.

By this time Andrew felt he had come home. He loved all of the Kashmiri people, the food and places, and was getting on famously with whoever he met, of whatever faith or persuasion. I was a little more circumspect, as it had been mentioned by our host that he hoped that the following morning we would take a 'short' seven-hour trip over the single main road to Srinagar by car for a quick look at the 'proper' Kashmir.

I wanted to decline due to tiredness (the wedding and its build-up of parties and engagements had been surprisingly exhausting for us) – and then there was the small consideration of the local news reports telling of repeated terrorist attacks on several passenger cars traveling that very route. In truth we never for a moment feared for our safety whilst we were in Kashmir or elsewhere in India, it was more a sense of going with the flow, but it just didn't 'feel' right at the time and I couldn't see us making that trip. So we didn't. It had now been five days since our preliminary visit to the holy men in Delhi and we had agreed to ring them to find out what progress had been made.

Unbeknown to us beforehand, however, it wasn't possible to make any long distance phone-calls from Kashmir as there was a Government restriction on usage – mobiles and landlines were used by terrorists, so the whole area was almost permanently blocked off to prevent any arrangements being made from outside (I guess they meant Pakistan). But our diplomacy at the wedding party paid off when on hearing of our plight, a new-found friend and politician we had met at the wedding kindly arranged to call Delhi on our behalf.

Yes, they had found Andrew's thumbprint! I had to laugh – he had only gone along with the whole business because I had wanted him to, and he had never for a moment thought he would be found, let alone be the first… But indeed, they had the bundles for his category in Delhi and were ready to confirm his next appointment, so I was really excited at the prospect of what was to come. A new adventure was about to unfold. Andrew was both blasé and guarded, seeing it now as a challenge with the gauntlet thrown down at him first; yet at the same time he was wondering just what he was about to be told. I sensed what he needed to know was about to be told whilst we were in India. We fixed his appointment for the Thursday, the day after we arrived back in Delhi.

CHAPTER TWO

Andrew's Date With Destiny

So will your leaf be there, waiting for you to come at the time it had appointed for you, millennia ago? Well, much to my dismay and surprise, mine was.

At that time I was not aware of much if anything that has been written in the preceding or the following pages. Had I been so I might well have bolted from the consulting room a great deal earlier with all I was told that day, and the implications and realizations that it held and would so violently kick-start in me immediately afterwards.

'Speak as you find' the saying goes, so I will. When Angela first mooted our possible detour to meet the Naadi readers in Tamil Nadu I was circumspect to say the least – it all sounded just too incredible to be taken seriously, all too illogical for words. However intriguing it was now to Angela and may have been for Deepak Chopra, I could not accept that any normal person could really believe that some ancient old sage sitting alone in a cave in India thousands of years ago should have felt inclined – let alone be able – to write down the detail of someone's life or lives, and the precise detail of my own life – an Englishman far ahead in the future – right up to the current date, and then cover his past and future lives as well. And get it all correct? Please.

But to keep Angela happy I'd agreed to go along with it if that was what she wanted, so long as we could manage to fit it in with the limited time that we had over there, my view being that we might just as well have two readings as one if it ever got that far. So if they found me, I would have my reading. But while somehow I felt sure Angela's would be found if anyone was, it never entered my head that I would be too – I felt smugly confident that was tempting fate a bit too far.

Yet here we were. We had given them our thumbprints, we'd been to the wedding, and here we were on the Thursday afternoon, back at the strange little Naadi establishment (I still don't know what to call it – it's not an office and it isn't a church, nor a shrine nor a chapel, more like a doctor's surgery), two floors above a shifty looking realtor's and next to a noisy vet's in the middle of Delhi's Krishna Market. I was standing on the dusty balcony once again, waiting to take off my shoes and enter to see if my leaf was there.

On the wall by the door I caught sight of a sign reading 'Thursday Holiday' in big letters... and just for an instant I thought I might get away with it – like missing a painful dental appointment through no fault of your own – but no, just my luck, the white-robed man we had met earlier came to let us in.

It was a moment of truth for sure.

Faith and trust have never been my strongest points. I've had many readings in my time: some good and some bad, some from fairground gypsies or those in psychic fairs, others from recognized, established international mediums like my Angela. And so far I'd managed to reason my way out of all of them, passing off any accurate messages merely as intuition, lucky coincidences or wishful thinking. But somehow this time it already felt very different and I had the strangest feeling that self-evidence was about to slap me hard in the face.

Whether it was the religious overtones – the pictures of the Hindu gods with their bright orange garlands decked about the walls, the holy man in white bowing solemnly as I came in, the muted chanting and prayers I could hear in a background room, or the ceremonial pots, pans and strange-looking produce held high on trays being taken through as offerings to the gods in the prayer room behind, or the otherwise quiet and tangible air of deep spiritual respect and seriousness the whole place exuded – whatever it was I really didn't know, but now I felt nervous, the arrogant skepticism I'd had up to then fast draining away. For the first time I found myself wondering whether any of this could possibly be true. Was my leaf really going to be here, and if so, what would it tell me?

I reached for Angela's hand, wishing all this was for her not me. She squeezed it, deeply curious, yet clearly enjoying my discomfort. For her this was payback time, the recompense for all my sarcasm over the years. I tried to smile but inside I felt like a lamb being sent off to slaughter.

With Elias acting as our interpreter the three of us were ushered through the empty waiting room into a tiny, enclosed side-room with a small table and three chairs. We sat down in silence and were left alone, the door closing quietly behind us. It was more like a cell than a room. There were no windows and it was stiflingly hot, with only a small fan to move the heavy, scented air. The light was dim, but I could see the many pictures of Hindu gods and saints – Ganesh, Shiva, Parvathi, Babaji, staring down at me, all fierce smiles, scowls and unblinking eyes – sitting on the shelving that ran around the walls, the burnt evidence of countless ceremonies scattered around the floor below them. A small bell sat on the table, with a battered tape recorder on the linoleum underneath, unplugged.

The Naadi reader came in. White-robed again, he was a short thick-set man in his early thirties, polite, friendly yet somewhat severe in appearance. He carried several bundles under his arm. He bowed and smiled, putting the bundles down on the desk and moving his hands to the Hindi position of welcome and prayer. He sat down and we introduced ourselves. Elias explained that he would translate whatever was said (in any language the holy man spoke) and would work the tape deck we had brought with us.

A flurry of Indian followed. No, the Naadi reader would record the session, but it would be the session that followed once my leaf had been found – much time and tape could be wasted beforehand, with little of it meaningful until my actual leaf was near, so any recording would be fruitless until later.

Through Elias he then recapped that the Naadi system divided all human souls into 108 basic categories covering the whole of mankind, so the first stage was to check which of the categories my thumbprint fell into – this was the process we had begun before leaving for Kashmir. Now we needed to find out whether my particular leaf was within one of the bundles of that category that he now had with him. He warned it may not be in any, saying it may not yet be the moment I was destined to meet with it, but I wasn't to worry as my leaf would surely make itself known and tell me if it was there.

He explained that the categories were classified by specific markings. Not the whole of the thumb (which the police would use for forensic evidence) but certain parts of it, where the line impressions and the dots held the most significant meanings. A dot placed here means one thing, two dots there means something else and so on. Every thumbprint will be unique, but by going through and checking each leaf within each bundle hopefully my leaf and I would be identified and reunited – done by telling me my race, creed, personality, family members and their names, my aims, jobs of work, career, loves, troubles and so on – so that afterwards my predictions and any remedies necessary to ward off ills or purge my ongoing sins could be prepared, based upon the fixed astronomical and astrological calculations that the Naadi reader would use …. I heard the word 'sins'. What sins? I wasn't aware of having any. But he was carrying on.

All I had to do was say 'Yes' or 'No' to his questions (via Elias) as he went through the bundles one leaf at a time. He neither wanted nor needed anything else to be said or proffered, so neither Angela nor I were to comment or divulge any details to him during the entire session. All that seemed clear enough, so I sat back and waited expectantly while he composed himself. I took a deep breath. It seemed my moment of truth had finally arrived.

With a muttered prayer to the gods we were off. Elias explained that the hushed words were the holy man humbly asking the goddess Parvati to intercede on my behalf with her husband Lord Shiva so that he would tell the reader what the great saint and prophet Kausika had faithfully recorded on my palm-leaf under his Lord's direction over two thousand years ago.

Carefully the reader unwrapped the first bundle, looking at Elias to translate.

Examples of leaves in bundles

The leaves he said, almost chanting his words, were written in the Tamil language and were the very words of Saint Kausika himself. He explained that he and the other Rishis (or Sris) had taken it upon themselves to set down what Shiva told them regarding the lives of everyone who lived, had lived or would ever live on Earth in their entirety.... and my leaf would be there if this was the time I was destined to meet it. I would know it when it came, but until then he would pass on each leaf every time I said 'no' to any question he asked me, for other lives were held on each leaf too... until such time as only mine remained.

He paused again.

By now all manner of thoughts were skipping unchecked through my mind, intrigued, fascinated and alarmed as it was, yet searching hard for any obvious trickery, loophole or way out it could find, suspicious to the last. 'The lives of everyone who lived, had lived or would ever live on Earth'.... How could that be possible? That would be billions of people. Nonsense. It was ridiculous. He couldn't be serious. How could my answers be noted or recorded? Was there some little scribe next door, listening, poised to write down whatever I said 'Yes' to, only to discreetly insert a wholly correct leaf into one of the bundles that would be opened later? Is that how they did it? I looked around, noting there were no vents through which a scribe could listen, no microphones or leads to another room, while the door onto the corridor outside our room was heavy, solid and closed. So could the reader himself be trained to remember every correct detail? I could only wait and see.

The reader started again, prefacing each question on the leaf with a sonorous chant in Tamil.

Naadi reader/Elias: *"Are you a Brahmin?"*

Me: "No." (He discards that leaf and moves onto the next.)

Naadi reader: *"Your mother is alive."*

Me: "Yes." (Good guess. He stays with the same leaf.)

Naadi reader: *"Your father is no more."*

Me: "Yes." (Good guess again.)

Naadi reader: *"Your father was a very good man."*

Me: "Yes." (Of course he was. We stay on that leaf.)

Naadi reader: *"Your mother was a housewife. She had no job."*

Me: "Yes." (I'm beginning to think this will be just like so many readings.)

Naadi reader: *"You have a technical job."*

Me: "No." (I had had until quite recently but not any longer. This leaf is discarded.)

Naadi reader: *"You have had several court cases."*

Me: "No." (Wrong again. I think he's just fishing but then, having thought about it, I remembered there could have been a case looming, but there hadn't been any to date. He moved on to the next leaf.)

That leaf was quickly discarded too. By the time he began on the second bundle. I wasn't over-impressed – it sounded like it was going to be an endless session of 'No' answers, more like 'Twenty Questions'.

Naadi reader: *"Your father was in defense."*

Me: "Er?... No." (A 'No' yet again, but unsure – what exactly did he

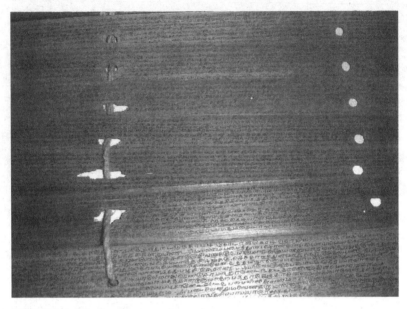

The leaves when unwrapped

mean? As he started to discard the leaf, Elias interrupted: "He means your father was in the Armed Services, that is what 'Defense' means here.")

Me: "Oh I see… Yes." (In fact the Royal Navy. He stays with that leaf.)

Naadi reader: *"Your mother is incurring medical expenses."*

Me: "Um… Yes." (She was in a private home.)

Naadi reader: *"She is a good woman."*

Me: "Yes." (Naturally.)

Naadi reader: *"You are running 55 years."*

Me: "No, I'm 54." (I knew I shouldn't have said that but it somehow seemed a small triumph until Elias interrupted again – "but on your next birthday you will be 55, no?")

Me: "Yes." (Point taken.)

Naadi reader: *"You have two vehicles."*

Me: "No." (He discards that leaf and starts the next.)

I was disappointed. I'd thought for a minute or two we had been getting somewhere with that last one. We went on, quickly finishing that bundle with my repeatedly telling him 'No'. We begin on the third bundle; I was feeling cocky – this was just like any other reading – and somehow I felt almost cheated. Was this all it would amount to? If so, how on earth had the great Deepak Chopra been so impressed?

Naadi reader: *"You are married."*

Me: "Yes." (That's obvious for goodness sake – who was I sitting there with?)

Naadi reader: *"You are divorced from first wife. Second marriage still going on."*

Me: "Yes." (Just a bit uncomfortable now. How could he know I'd been married before? Another good guess, or had Elias told him?)

Naadi reader: *"You have one sister."*

Me: "No." (Wrong yet again! He moves to the next leaf.)

Naadi reader: *"You have no sisters."*

Me: "Correct." (He's quick!)

Naadi reader: *"You have one brother."*

Me: "No." (By now I'm getting very cynical. He starts to discard the leaf, then stops, re-reads a section and looks up at me.)

Naadi reader: "You *had* one brother…"

Me: "Eh? What? No." (Then, as he starts to discard the leaf I remember what my mother had told me years back. I did have an older brother, or would have had one called Angus had he not died two years before I was born. I sit back, now a bit sheepish and rather stunned. The reader smiles politely and goes back to the same leaf.)

Naadi reader: *"You are married now for over 11-12 years. Your life is going smoothly."*

Me: "Yes."

Naadi reader: *"Your wife's name is Anja-ler."* (His pronunciation is labored but then I'm no good at Indian names either.)

Me: "Yes." (I smile. He'd heard me call Angela by name when we introduced ourselves.)

Naadi reader: *"Your wife is a very good person with great talent. A very good positive thinker, well educated, doing creative work and also doing writing work."*

Me: "Yes." (Can't argue with any of that.)

Naadi reader: *"You have no children."*

Me: "Yes."

Naadi reader: *"You have recently moved house – a very good move – 8 or 9 months ago. Very happy move for you."*

Me: "Yes." (I was taken aback. How true that was. I begin to feel a good bit more uncomfortable.)

Naadi reader: *"You have drastically changed job – last year. Summer. Now new career."*

Me: "Yes." (Spot on.)

Naadi reader: *"You are doing private job now."*

Me: "Eh?" (Elias interrupted: 'he means working for yourself.')

Me: "Yes."

Naadi reader: *"You are writing for yourself and doing some kind of video and audio work."*

Me: "Why yes…" (I'm staggered – it was exactly right – Angela and I had been writing documentary and entertainment formats for TV and I was writing a book as well…. But how would Kausika possibly know about 'video' or 'audio' back then in his cave, before electrics, recorders, tape or film or any of that?)

Naadi reader: *"You went to university and have a degree."*

Me: "Yes." (I'm impressed, but try to think it could just be another good guess)

Naadi reader: *"A degree in Arts… and a Masters."*

Me: "Yes." (Now I'm listening hard.)

Naadi reader: *"In Archee-tech-ture."*

Me: (My breath stops short, I'm blown away.) "Yes" I stammer. (I had been an architect for nearly thirty years with a degree and a Masters, but had never thought any of it showed.)

And so it went on until we'd been on that leaf for a good while longer. It was starting to sound like a procession of 'yes's' to every question he asked, so by now I was feeling about two inches tall and sitting very still and quiet, my mouth dropped open in silent amazement. I was also beginning to think the unthinkable: does this mean my leaf is near? Could it even be the one he's on now? The reader continued.

Naadi reader: *"Your father's name begins with a T."*

Me: "Yes." (I'm amazed all over again.)

Naadi reader: *"His name was Timo-tee."*

Me: "Yes." (Aghast.)

Naadi reader: *"Your mother's name begins with a D."*

Me: "Yes." (Listening extremely closely now and not breathing at all.)

Naadi reader: *"Her name is Doro-tee."*

Me: "Yes." (Even more aghast.)

Naadi reader: *"It is predicted on the leaf that you would come at this age and time."*

Me: (I found myself laughing delightedly, and with great pleasure. Yes, it felt true, it did – but how did it know?) "I guess it was."

The Naadi reader stopped and looked up. I looked back at him, watchful, not dismissive at all by now and feeling exhausted. We had been there for nearly an hour, yet the time had flown. To everything he was asking me I could now only answer 'Yes'. We ran through several more questions on that same leaf just in case – they were all 'Yes's' from me, of course – and then he stopped, smiling broadly, saying he was satisfied that we had finally found it. My leaf was there.

I sat there trying to take it all in and make sense of it. By now we had covered my parents, family, background, education, profession, wives, working career, homes, health, possessions, ambitions, relationships, abilities, talents, children, the time and date of my birth and the day of the week it fell on (I checked afterwards, and of course it was the day he had said), my various illnesses, operations and accidents, even touching on old girlfriends and interests... every single detail of it was collected and written down on that one single leaf, and all of it was totally correct....

... I couldn't have assembled such a composite list if I'd tried – it was too complete, too focused, too accurate. I felt exactly like a bug pinned on a frame in the Natural History Museum: exposed, vulnerable and trapped, naked for all to see. And however unbelievable it sounded, at the same time it was clear that this was no 'memory man' or other such scam.

The sheer depth and range of the very many – way too many – intimate and personal details that he had come up with, and which only I myself had known, were far too secret, unusual and extensive for even the most brilliant guesswork or process of lucky elimination. No one could hold and discover such an extent of such deeply held personal knowledge about me in so short a time unless it was as it was – already written down on that leaf in front of him.

Without a doubt it was Round One to the Naadis. I simply couldn't believe it. That leaf lying on the table in front of me was *me* and no one else. That was my soul's DNA sitting there. I'd heard it all emerge, piece by piece, word by word exactly as my identity slowly took shape and crystallized. How *could* it be so from a thumbprint alone? I looked at Angela, my mind a blank, truly glad she was there. She smiled and squeezed my hand, well aware of the great shock I was in.

Unsteadily, I got up and lurched towards the door – I badly needed to get out of there and have a smoke. I needed to think. That leaf had been written thousands of years ago, then copied and recopied as its natural structure had perished over time, in order for it to be preserved and retained until such time as I appeared to meet up with it, countless centuries later... at that moment only, not a day earlier. It was beyond any reality or credibility that I could give it, yet it was there, I'd heard it all for myself, point by point. It was crystal clear that only that leaf and I knew all the secrets of what it had held. No one else could or would have dovetailed with it so very exactly, in every detail possible.

Never had I had such a session as that before. My mind was numb, my head whirled and my eyes took nothing in. Together we stumbled outside to the balcony, leaving Elias with the reader packing up the bundles.

Once outside, in desperation I asked Angela whether Elias could possibly have told the reader all about me beforehand. (Why is it people always assume psychics have the time or ability to do detailed research on the complete strangers they meet?) She just looked at me, disappointed, reminding me that Elias had not met the reader before and anyway, Elias didn't know a small fraction of what had been revealed to us in that room – how could he? – even she hadn't known a lot of it.

And nor had I, I realized, until that leaf had told me of so many things that had been long-buried or past. I know it may sound silly to you, reading this, but I was knocked sideways by all that had been said and by what had happened so far. As I think I've made clear, I'm not one who readily goes along with all this sort of thing (even if I am lucky enough to be married to an attractive, fun-loving and big-hearted medium) and I had been expecting little more than a few general, easy-to-dismiss and simple-to-follow platitudes which no doubt would have sufficed for most of us in terms of a 'reading'.

I hadn't bargained on getting what I'd just heard, not for a second. As I stood out there on the balcony, I really was having trouble coming to terms with the fact that not only was my life's history (to date) set down and fully covered on that one individual leaf, but it had all been written down – and so mapped out for me – all those years ago. Where was 'I' in all this? What choices did I have in any of it? Where was my free will if everything I'd done so far had already been known about and pre-ordained? Were we all pre-destined?

* * *

"Well that's it," I was thinking (in mental panic) as I puffed away, leaning over the balcony, staring stupidly into space and trying to get a grip. "I've done it and it's over. Someone else can be found now… please let it be Angela. She can deal with this so much better than I can – I'm not up to it." Believe it or not I had begun to feel guilty. Having been so flippant and scathingly dismissive about the whole business right from the start, it seemed somehow very wrong if I was now the only one to be found among the bundles. Angela had believed in it, she had pushed hard for it and had always deserved a reading far more than me, the perennial doubting-Thomas. I'd had my fingers burnt quite enough already, thank you: the damp squib I'd expected had turned out to be white hot and deadly accurate.

By now, Elias had come out and joined us. He peered at me strangely, looking for my reactions. He grinned and slapped me hard on the back. "Pretty good, eh?" he bellowed. But behind the bravado I could see he was impressed and taken aback at the extent of what he had heard and translated.

"And now for the rest," he added archly. "Your Predictions and your Remedies. He says he'll need about 30 or 40 minutes to do your chart."

'Predictions?' 'Remedies?' What 'chart?' Inside I grew frantic all over again, worried and perplexed as I listened to Elias while talking to Angela, steered away no doubt by the wild look he'd seen in my eyes. It seems he had asked the Naadis for the full service – my past life and my future life as well, and this was what the reader was now transcribing. Based on the information given on my leaf, my identity had been established and therefore my recent and future soul's history could also be accessed and be told to me in much the same way, as it would in just a few moments time. My knees went weak at the thought and my stomach rebelled. I had expected to be back at the hotel by now, with a stiff drink in my hand. How I wanted that.

Angela tried to comfort me while we waited for what else was to come.

* * *

Although I didn't know it then, the philosophy behind the leaves is made up of the *Naadi Granthas*, a set of very highly organized manuscripts each comprising between 16 and 24 chapters, called *Kandams*. The number of chapters depends upon which Naadi astrologer you go to, as each of the original *Sapta Rishis,* the Seven Sages credited with being the very first to inscribe and record them thousands of years ago has their own following – Agasthya, Kausika, Vyasa, Bohar, Bhrigu, Vasishtha and Valmiki. Their names seem to vary depending upon which source you read; I have since come across other names such as Athri, Parasara, Jaya-Muni, Bhujandar, Vidura and Narada.

Suffice it to say that particular *Granthas* deal with particular issues – the *Satya Naadi* deals with the lives of the great and the good, the truly outstanding and world-renowned persons in whatever field, whilst the *Kaka Bhujandar Naadi* concentrates solely on future world events. There are basically two types of Naadi astrology – the *Tantra* Naadi, those that use and deal with horoscopes, and the *Mantra* Naadi, who rely on a few simple questions and answers only, from which the Naadi reader will make his pronouncements, and which surely must therefore be limited and open to question. My reading was both – extensive questioning to find my leaf and then my horoscope chart based on the precise date and time of my birth.

Each *Kandam* or chapter relates to a specific aspect of a person's material and spiritual life, and thanks to Elias I was going to receive guidance on all of the 16 Chapters that our Naadis practiced – Kausika Naadi; *Kandams* 1-12 had already been covered in my reading so far, and would now be expanded with my Predictions, while *Kandams* 13-16 would be dealt with in the Remedies in whatever appropriate form was then found necessary.

* * *

On hearing what Elias had said I thought I would never escape, I was never going to get away. It seemed things could only get more alarming still for me, like being at the dentist's when he's found there is a mouthful of painful work to be done before you will be free to leave.

After what seemed like an eternity to me, the reader called us back in. He was now very much more relaxed and was clearly delighted that my leaf and I had been reunited. In fact, he acted more like a midwife who had successfully delivered a baby to its mother than the dentist poised to inflict punishment. I smiled nervously at him.

We went back in and sat down again, in a larger room this time, right at the back of the building, with a single large window and a hefty drop outside – so no chance for any eavesdropping from there.

Even more gods stared down at me from the walls, sitting above piles of empty ceremonial pots, stacks of old newspapers and bags of grain. Another tape deck sat on the windowsill with a stack of unopened tapes beside it. He unwrapped a tape and inserted it; then, after switching the recorder on and composing himself, we were off once more. There was more sonorous chanting but this time he didn't expect me to say a word. He re-introduced me to Lord Shiva by re-confirming my identity and seeking his permission and help to relay the details of my past and future lives to me, including any sins I still had running on.

There it was again – my 'sins'. I licked my dry lips, wondering what they could be… I didn't need all that as well, not right now. Angela grinned, clearly most curious and intrigued. I tried to relax, my fleeting thoughts telling me that I had committed none at all, or none of any consequence, having been at pains in my life to do just the opposite whenever temptation arose, I surely rationalized. So it would be all right then, wouldn't it?

The reader started again, with Elias translating:

"Lord Shiva states for you, Andrew, as Sri Kausika has written: 'Meru', 'Denar', 'Reika', meaning 'mountain', 'money',' lines'. It is written for you name, fame, money – which you will get when you are older. You are trying for this now; it will come, but later."

He followed this introduction with my birth date in both Hindi and Tamil, then gave my birth sign and the details of my astrological chart from which he had calculated my horoscope. He paused before carrying on.

"The two dots on your thumb print are a first quality impression. This means you are knowledgeable and intelligent and progressing every year."

Then he recapped my basic details, as if from a list:

"You are running 55 years."

"You were supposed to come at this age and time to predict the future."

"Your father is no more – his name is Timothy – he was in Defense. Your father was a very good man."

"You had one brother, he is no more. You have no living brothers or sisters."

"Your mother is alive – her name is Dorothy – God's blessings are on her. You have medical expenditure on her. She is dangerously ill at this moment, near death, but she will recover – to save her you must make a donation to her favorite charity."

I jerked back. True, my mother had been ill when we'd left for India, but not dangerously so, and certainly not *near death*. Angela and I exchanged an anxious glance.

"You got married. You are divorced from your first wife."

"Seconnd marriage is still going on. Your wife's name is Angela."

"You have been married for 11-12 years and life is going smoothly."

"Your wife is a very good person with great talent, very good positive thinker, also well educated in creative work and is also doing writing work."

"You have had a good education. You have a Degree in Arts, a Masters – some kind of architecture. You had your own business but have recently drastically changed your job. Now you do some kind of audio/video work and presently you are writing – this is a private job."

"Your profile shows you are much more talented than you are showing

presently. At times people are jealous of you. You are writing well – you will be very satisfied with your writing; there is promotion, money and sudden luck. You will have success and settle in business."

"Your wife is your working partner; you will have no other partner – no outsiders."

"You have changed homes in eight or nine months from now, locally – a very good change."

"You will have medical money expenditure soon. Stomach operation. It will be all right."

I jerked back again. Apart from the surprises and shocks I was having from the reading, I felt perfectly all right, and had been so for many months. Not even a cold. Little did I know. He paused and looked at me. Elias explained we had reached the stage covering my most recent 'past life'. He went on:

"In your last life you have done some sins, and in this life also – too many to talk about. You are carrying sins from your first marriage also, loads of them. You will have to do a prayer to make everything right for you."

I was shocked. I was convinced I'd done no such thing, and certainly not in my last marriage. I hadn't broken it up. Before I could interject he carried on.

"In your last life you were born in a 'Kshatriya' family, people who were fighters. You were a warrior, a powerful man. Your name was Loaknat. You were in love with a Brahmin girl of the highest caste. You loved her but did not marry her, you left her and she cursed you – affecting your health. You then married another woman and had two children, but gave them pain and left them too. They cursed you as well – this is the reason why you can have no children now. These four people cursed you."

The bluntness of his last sentences was another body blow. I was horrified to think I'd been cursed. Then again, I'd never been desperate to have children, more like the opposite in fact, but deep inside what he said closed a circuit, it rang true, it felt right, it explained and made sense of so many things that hadn't made any real sense to me before.

"You had done all these things when you were middle-aged in your last life, but when you grew older you started doing very good work and helping poor people, which is why you have the good birth that you have now, this time. But you are still carrying your last life's curses, which is why you have had failure in your first marriage, no children, some health problems and no success in your mind and heart. We will give you the Remedy to clear them."

I was very relieved to hear it. Then, just as I started to feel a bit better about it all, he hit me with the coup de grace, the knockout punch.

"Later you will try adopting a child – again – and be successful. This child, a boy, will be very lucky for you. He and your wife will look after you well."

I couldn't have said a word if I'd wanted to. Slowly I just looked across at Angela. It was that word '*again*' that did it, for both of us. How could anyone, let alone dear old Kausika all those thousands of years ago, know that Angela and I had – very discreetly and very privately – tried to adopt a child some years before but had been unsuccessful due to the endless red tape that had been thrown in our way. So perhaps we had not been truly earnest enough at the time, but nevertheless we had quietly talked about doing it again later, when and if we were better able and equipped to do so. Yet up until that very instant that the reader spoke, no one else save Angela and I had known of our proposal to do any such thing – we had deliberately told no one.

He then summed up with a very positive prediction:

"You will have name and fame. You will have a great following from the younger generation. Kids will follow your writing – you will write stories on the gods."

And that was pretty well it. Which was just as well. Even though he still had to tell me what my future held, Round Two and the whole Contest as far as I was concerned had gone without any doubt to the

Naadis. I was a beaten man, knocked out by the knowledge of me that only I – and the leaf in front of me – knew to be the truth.

* * *

Before I mention the Predictions covering the rest of my life (this lifetime), let me give you the full list of the 16 *Kandams* that were covered when we had our Naadi readings. I have set them down exactly as they were written on the inside cover of the booklet I was given by the Naadi reader, along with the tape recording of my reading, these two representing the formal record of all that I was told:

List of Kandams
1. To be found out through thumb impression (Gents' Right: Ladies' Left) or horoscope of the concerned person. Will contain name, parents' name, present details of profession, brothers, sisters, children, wife and gist of future predictions for all the 12 houses in the horoscope based on planetary positions.
2. Money, Eyes, Family, Education and Speech.
3. Number of brothers and sisters, Affection, help and ill-feeling in between self and brothers and sisters. Ears, Courtage, House and Pleasures.
4. Mother, House, Vehicles, Land & Pleasures.
5. Children, Birth, Death, reason for not having children, adoption of remedial measures for having children, future lives of the children.
6. Disease, Debts, Enemies & Court cases, Remedial measures for avoidance and success.
7. Time of marriage, Place, Name, Lagnam. Planetary position of the bride or bridegroom. Future life with husband or wife.
8. Longvity (sic), Accident & danger to life, Age, month, date, day, time star, lagnam and place of death.

9. Father – predictions in regard to father, wealth, visit to temples, Luck, Preaching through holy men, charitable deeds.
10. Profession, Future prediction in regards to job or business. Change of place, good effects & evils in profession.
11. Profit and second marriage.
12. Expenditure, Foreign visit, next birth & Attainment of Salvation.

Separate Kandams

13. Santi Pariharam: Last birth, Sins committed, remedial measures for getting rid of the effect of past birth's sins.
14. Deeshai Pariharam: Manthra Jebam, wearing of Rakshai (Talisman) for avoidance of enemy's troubles, Jaddu, Tona etc...
15. Oushada Kandam: Medicines for long-standing diseases and method (sic) of taking the medicines.
16. Dasa Bukthi Kandam: Predictions for the running Dasa Bukthi (Major and Subperiods of planetary movements).

Note: (i) Kandams (Chapters) 2 to 12 will give the future predictions up to end of the life from the date of reading the Kandam.

(ii) Other than the above Kandams there are Ganga Kandam, Prasna Kandam, Dasa Bukthi Santhi Kandam and Politics & Political Career Kandam

So this was what comprised the whole service that Elias had commissioned for me. While the first Kandam is clearly more of a general introduction, when you look at the breadth and depth of the information all 16 Chapters are intended to provide, it doesn't leave much to the imagination. Small wonder I felt drained and bedazzled with the extent of detail I had been given.

The Naadi reader then told me what the rest of my present life holds for me in two-yearly tranches, from 'running 55' until running to my early 80s, with each of the significant moments outlined and highlighted throughout. And while there obviously remains a very great deal that has yet to be proven to me (or to anyone else), with all that had been said and gone before, how could I now possibly doubt the truth of any of it? And all gleaned from three thumbprints, your gender, and a Christian name.

Two of these predictions proved to be true quite swiftly.

When we got back to our hotel that evening I was handed a note at the desk. It was a call from my mother's residential home requesting that I ring them immediately. I did so, only to learn that my mother was 'very dangerously ill' and asking me to return to the UK as quickly as possible. I told them we were due to fly back in 48 hours. With some awkwardness, they asked whether I had a particular undertaker in mind, hence the urgency of their request for me to return, which made the shock even greater. I stammered a few words, remembering the donation I now had to make and quickly, which I did immediately on our return. And desperately ill as she was then, she recovered to live another year.

By now the whole shocking effect of my Naadi reading had taken a hard grip on me, working at some deep level I had not even imagined let alone understood. I became ill almost as soon as we reached the hotel, probably the catharsis of the shock brought on by the reading and the news of my mother's state, leaving me unable to hold onto what I had eaten. Angela summoned the hotel doctor the following morning, who prescribed some pills he was sure would work, but in fact they made no difference at all. The long night flight home was a nightmare, as were the few short weeks that followed as the weight continued to fall off me. I thought I had dysentery, but my doctor thought otherwise and managed slowly to get it under control.

Not that this is in any way important save that in his examination of me he found I had developed a bad hernia, for which I had to go into hospital immediately if it was to be treated in time. The Naadi's words echoed in my ears: *"You will have medical money expenditure soon. Stomach operation. It will be all right."* And so it was.

One further point about that: when the reader had reached the point in my life that was ten years ahead, when I was 'running 65', he had told me I would have to have another *"stomach operation, for same reason… It will be all right also"*. It had made no sense to me at the time of course but, as I was leaving the clinic after the hernia operation, the surgeon jokingly said he'd see me in ten years time, "when the mesh needs to be replaced". I grinned stupidly back him, for the moment utterly thrown, but by the time I was in the car going home I was surprised the Naadi reader hadn't given me the surgeon's name as well.

But I'm running too far ahead. As we left the Naadis late that afternoon, Angela was told that her leaf had also been found (to much relief and rejoicing all round) and that she would have her reading before I was given my Remedies the following day – 'remedies' being the *'puja'* or prayers and offerings that I had to make if I was to atone for the many sins I still carried and so clear my present life of the bad elements that would otherwise frustrate the happy path ahead that I had been told of and given in my reading.

Naturally we quickly both agreed to return the following afternoon.

CHAPTER THREE

Angela's Reading: Knowing and Believing

Since spending so many hours with the 'Tamil Ola Readers', as I now call them, I have had much time to absorb the whole awe-inspiring effect on Andrew and myself. There is an amazing sense of timelessness and a peaceful calm emanating from deep within the holy men themselves, but I feel it is also due to the dedication of their life's work solely for the benefit of the vast array of people who come to find their life's purpose through them.

It is an extremely clever set-up whichever way you look at it. From a reason and logic point of view, the recipient is first hit with a considerable number of home-truths, then subjected to an onslaught of verbal and mental self-punishments regarding their past sins. All of which ties in neatly with the blocks and problems that have taken place up to that very moment in the recipient's life, so that – when they finally pick themselves up off the floor – they are extremely grateful to be offered the 'get out of jail card free' provided they are prepared to begin doing penance (by prayer or *puja*) and making payback immediately, and if they are lucky enough that their list of sins isn't too great.

Now this is when it starts to get interesting. Because if there is plenty *puja* to do we are talking of at least a year or more to clear the way for your life to improve, during which time the person has to personally do daily prayers to atone for their sins, as well as give to the poor or to charity. All of this goes on whilst the Brahmin priests in Tamil Nadu chant and carry out ritualistic prayers on your behalf, sometimes as many as five times a day for the period of time deemed necessary to ameliorate or eradicate your sins.

So with all that is involved I can't imagine many people in the western world would be ready to even consider a visit to the Naadis unless they felt they were already holier than thou!

As a spiritual medium, I have already learnt to work with my sensitivity and this has benefited me greatly throughout my life. The self-evidence has built up and strengthened me over time, and I know well to trust the order of events, as I firmly believe I am responsible and have been the co-creator in all of them.

* * *

So what was told to me? Well, finding my leaf didn't take long. The holy man bought in four bundles, each wrapped with strings that looked very frayed. Once opened, the individual leaves looked old and worn in the center where the strings went through, leaving ragged, big holes in some, smaller in others... I kept thinking maybe the important bits will have worn away and he won't be able to read it all! But of course we were expected – and that really made me smile.

I hardly looked up whilst the holy man went through my life. Amazingly, all of the names he gave me were correct first time. Then I noticed my bundles were small by comparison with Andrew's so, logic playing its part, did that mean there was so little so say about my own life? It only seemed as though a short time passed, maybe only half an hour, before I had said 'Yes' to everything. Some of the salient points of the reading went like this:

"You are the middle of your parent's children"

I was, I beat my younger sister by 20 minutes.

"You are a twin – one of twin sisters."

Correct.

"Your mother and father have expired, your mother then later your father."

My mother passed in 1991 and my father in 2003.

"One sister, your second sister, is still alive, very well educated; she has one son, who studied well and is doing well."

Correct.

"Your twin sister died in early middle age with health problems; she was not married."

Correct. This gave me a moment of sadness to hear it being said to me, the connection was so great between us.

"You had one brother who expired early on."

Correct. He passed at birth.

"You have had two marriages, the first marriage was a failure; it cost you a lot of money in divorce through the courts."

Whoops, spot on! Feels like another lifetime ago now.

"Your second marriage is very good."

Correct. Although I felt that is pretty obvious to me and others around us, it was great to have it said and think that it was written thousands of years ago.

I have to confess all that was being said pinpointed my life extraordinarily accurately right up to the moment that I sat there, so I became increasingly excited to hear what he was going to tell me about my past life or lives. I have always believed that most humans hold knowledge in their memories affecting their present lives. Somehow 'past baggage' answers that for me, while a 'collective memory' just doesn't do it. There are fears born in people, so where do they come from, if not from a past life? I am sure that the memory bank from past lives can be tapped and, if necessary, healed as well.

Andrew – who was very pale and drawn by then – was definitely looking forward to hearing my next session reveal all, hoping to get his own back. Not that I could blame him after what he had been through the day before, let alone the *puja* ceremony he was going to have to start when I was through. I hoped he would be feeling a bit better by then.

An hour went by, waiting in the sweltering heat of the afternoon. Then I was called back in. I almost had to trip Andrew up to stop him getting in before me, so anxious was he to hear my sins – we must have seemed like children.

Here are some of them...

"13th Chapter – previous birth details:

Lord Shiva – predictions and remedies, to get rid of all sins and curses on Angela.

It was written that you would come at this time and age.

Your last life was in Singapore over 150 years ago.

Islam was your religion.

You were a Muslim girl from a very good Muslim family – very cultured.

You were the first child.

Your name was Monisha.

You were a housewife.

You did not help or look after your parents.

You caused a lot of trouble to your husband up to middle age (before 30 years of age).

Then you became very good and started doing everything for them.

That is why you have a good life now.

You are still carrying some sins from then with you."

Having listened to all this it somehow made sense. After all, as I gave thought to my life today I realized I'd been playing out the same kind of rebellion right up to the age of 29 or 30. Was I repeating my past? I'd had many ups and downs trying to create some sort of order out of chaos, knowing all along that I was to live and work my spiritual path, but of course I still wanted everything and had been trying to balance my desires for fun, travel, family and love-life with my spiritual work and big business all at once – and it just didn't gel.

I had had my own company, then after that I had become managing director of a financial corporation, not because I was looking for it, but because it was offered to me on a plate. I simply couldn't resist it, being a 'queen bee' instead of a 'worker bee', and I suppose I just got used to all the trimmings. But eventually more and more my staff had been rushing around arranging sessions for me not as the 'boss' but as a medium, seeing people in the boardroom out-of-hours! I had always loved the spiritual work, yet I couldn't get my head round living the successfully materialistic life I was used to, or how I could do what I knew was truly right for me, my life's work, and survive financially. It was only when I reached 30 that I started to turn the corner and major alterations came into play to help, and from then on I had begun to follow the road to trust and allow.

All this was running through my mind as the predictions began.

"Sri Kausika has written about Angela's predictions....

Name of her thumbprint: Korbray Raika – 'Tower of the Temple'.

Highest point of the tower – 'Article Tower'.

Two dots in thumbprint means heart very good, very intelligent, very kind person, believes in God, very straightforward person.

Born in to a very respected cultured family.

Mother and father were very good, very intelligent, with helping minds and helpful to other people.

God's blessings are with you and he is very happy with you.

You are very calm and satisfied with life.

You have a lot of speech power and whatever you say has a lot of power.

It was written here in your leaf that you were going to see the Naadi of your life for your predictions now – that is why you are here."

I have to say I loved that. Since reaching 35 years old I had understood and accepted that our lives are written in advance of time. I just wish it didn't upset people so much to see it that way – but to be fair, it took me years of self-evidence to acknowledge this consciously.

"2004 – Your husband was in construction work then he did other work and now he is doing a writing career."

Absolutely spot-on... I could only smile at this statement.

"2005 – You will have a minor skin problem, but all will be ok."

"2006 – you will have minor skin problem again but there will be a remedy for you."

I forgot all about this as the months went by. Then I flew to New York, came back for a week and had to fly back out there again to do some filming. On the day I arrived back my fingers were itching. I had a look and found I had some sort of allergic reaction where my rings were; they became red, blistered and swollen. I kept my rings off but it took four or five months to heal the problem and then I had to be careful for a year with jewellery on that one hand. Very strange considering I had never had a skin problem in my life up to then. Still the same skin problem reared up again in 2006 and the jewellery is definitely staying in the box until I have sorted the problem.

"2006 – You will have a family agreement."

I had no idea what that could be, till I went through the tape for this book. Suddenly it dawned on me that I had several months ago made an agreement with my older sister over some wild native ponies that were heading for the meat market. We rescued them with the aid of a charity and I had agreed to keep and train them. The day I am writing this I moved three of them to my sister's place with the idea that she could now keep and look after them – it was our agreement. Now this may not sound much to you the reader, but I can assure you my sister and I hardly ever meet – only four times in 15 years and then for as little time as possible. Communication has been always been minimal.

"2007/8 – You will travel to many foreign countries and meet many famous and very good people. All you do will be successful and your speech will have power. All you say will be taken as words of wisdom and respect."

Oh yeah…?

"2010 – You will adopt a boy. It might be from one of your relations."

This I just knew had to come up if there was any truth in the predictions we had heard in Andrew's reading. But even so, somehow it was a surprise.

Then there was much more information covering significant details in one or two year lumps, up to my passing when I'm in my late 80s.

In many ways my reading was no surprise to me, perhaps because there was a sense of knowing already about it deep down inside. But to have your life read back to you as I had, is inevitably going to have some effect on you, whoever you are. For me it strongly resonated very deep in my soul, to the extent that at the time I felt I was re-living it again and at times I had feelings of great pain and sadness that are difficult to express, albeit they had a clearing and cleansing effect as well. I am sure what we hear or see, naturally hits us on various levels whether emotionally, physically, mentally or spiritually. For me it was very much a deeply spiritual awakening.

A short time after my session I paid a small amount of rupees to the holy men for the items they had to purchase on my behalf for the *puja* work. I joined Andrew in the *puja* room and we started an hour's ritual of prayers and offerings to all the Hindu gods. While I was involved in my own ceremony I found myself questioning the reason in my thoughts for the offerings to each of the gods and what was actually taking place on a spiritual level.

It dawned on me later that the gods held the key to our sins and it was in their hands to allow the sins we had to be purged and released – or not. I later became convinced that the gods had a real knowing as to whether or not we were genuinely repentant. Some of the gods are, to my mind, quite off-putting, not only visually but also in the mythical stories told about their lives – in other words they don't appear exactly squeaky clean or wholly altruistic or beneficent themselves! Trials and tribulations, jealousy and in-fighting all seem to be commonplace in the myths and stories about them. So it seems they are doing the only job of work they could be doing, given that their sins often match our own.

But if any of them were a door-keeper to the underworld (where I perceive such things as sins to be held) he or she would logically be the one that would permit your sins to be lifted out of the box and cleared or forgiven, based on your sincerity in seeking forgiveness.

Well, there was no question of my sincerity, or Andrew's for that matter, of that I am certain. In one way it seems not unlike the Roman

Catholic system of confession and forgiveness. Having been educated at a convent I could not imagine anything more guilt-ridden than that, and indeed the fears they breed in you are rife, so maybe the ancient Hindu system ticks a good many more positive boxes for me after all.

At the end of the *puja* ceremony I was told to be aware of the moon cycles as the new moon is a positive time for me and would greatly enhance my success. For your benefit I have included these cycles as they affect all living beings and life forms, and can give your life a boost as well:

THE FULL MOON

Is good for all types of power raising in your life including:

Calling in Protection
Working with Divination
Planning anything
Releasing something or someone
Working on anything in the past

THE BEST RESULTS CAN BE OBTAINED:
three days prior to the full moon
the night of the full moon
three days following the full moon

THE NEW MOON

Is good for new beginnings like:

Wishing for your own personal growth
Healing yourself or others
Starting a new venture or project (results start showing by the full moon)

The reading of my own personal 'ola of divine prophecy' was a deeply inspiring experience that touched my soul. I found myself questioning the very essence of the work these holy men were doing. Then I remembered that they were well aware (as was written) that they should come forward now and speak more publicly, they told us this is the moment in time that was written for them and humanity to meet in this way.

To me their energy fields exude a spirituality that comes from communing with the higher powers, or as they would say the gods. So to me they are like highly trained mediums, communing with the Source and tuning-in to connect with the Lords via the Naadi readers. These Lords are also the keepers of the underworld that holds all sins, curses and wrong-doings of humanity. So if I am right then Lord Shiva is acting as a bridge between these two worlds – not forgetting it is Shiva, I believe, who requested and received permission for the information on each of us to be read from the Akashic Records some 5,000 years ago.

Lord Shiva received the story of all creation and we mere mortals are now receiving a small but valuable understanding of his endeavors. Like so much that has been lost or forgotten in the eons of time, it is only a shimmering light in the distance, but is definitely in view. If we can at least grasp this understanding and then grab hold of it, people may eventually accept death as easily as they accept 'life. More importantly, people would also start to appreciate the incredible opportunity offered by recalling a life at another time. This greater truth of knowledge of our lives would make an incredible difference – as I know from experience.

The Naadi readings can strongly assist us all, as we two have found out only too clearly. It may be a truly shocking, cathartic experience that shakes you to the very core. But if by clearing your past 'baggage' through recognition of your sins and the *puja* work you have to do to release them, you can find a sense of peace and calm to receive limitless and boundless success, fun, health, wealth, gratitude and happiness – then what more can you ask?'

With my reading and *puja* now over, it was time for Andrew to find out about the Remedies he would need to purge his sins, worried as he was about the 'plenty *puja*' he would get for what he had done before...

CHAPTER FOUR

Andrew's Remedies: Correcting the Past

I'd had a rough night. In fact I felt I'd had a pretty bad time of it ever since I'd left the Naadis late the day before. First there had been the shock of the extent of secrets revealed by the complete stranger who had given me my reading, then the bad news about my mother, and then my sudden inability to eat or wander further than ten feet from a restroom once back in the hotel or anywhere else. So the prospect of receiving the 'Remedies' that would purge my ongoing sins was by now a very welcome one: I was well aware of how badly I needed them.

Yet getting my remedies had by now become a daunting prospect in itself – what further punishment was in store for me given the nature of my sins and the cold, clinical way in which they had been exposed? With Angela tagging along, I was led shame-faced into the tiny *puja* room, feeling like a prisoner awaiting sentence.

It turned out to be the same small windowless room in which my leaf finding had taken place. So the very same gods stared back at me and the scatterings of more offerings lay all over the floor: bits of singed coconut shell, leaves, fruits, petals, rice, charcoal, charred clothing – whatever it took, so it seemed. The room was obviously a well-used place. It was just as airless, stuffy and stiflingly hot as it had been before. Several candles were poised ready, and strong incense pervaded the air. To me it seemed very much like a tiny womb where you would be reborn once the sins were taken from you.

The reader beckoned us to sit. This was tricky given the room was so small and had only three chairs and a table for four people – Angela, Elias, myself and the reader, so we ignored the chairs and the three of us ended up sitting awkwardly on the floor. I sat with my back to one wall and my legs out in front with the soles of my feet pointing out at the holy man who stood in front of us. Elias hissed in my ear that this was a sign of grave and great dishonor to him, so I quickly hid my soles under the table.

The reader explained that, had we been staying in India for longer, within nine days I would have been expected to attend and do *puja* on an ongoing daily basis, but as we were due to fly out the following day it had been arranged that the Naadi holy men back in Tamil Nadu would make atonement and carry out the chants and prayers on my behalf in my absence, provided I now made obeisance to my past-life leaf, intoned the introductory prayers and arranged with them to do whatever else my *puja* required.

I had the sudden, ignoble, fleeting thought that this was perhaps how the Naadis really made their money, but just as quickly dismissed it. Daring Providence like that, in the presence of a holy man who took it all extremely seriously, seemed like pushing my luck just too far, especially after all that had been foretold by him the day before. I readily agreed – what other option was there if damnation and an unhappy life ahead were to be avoided? It seemed little enough for the rewarding, life-changing returns it all promised.

It turned out I was not going to get away quite that easily, however. He repeated it was vital that I performed the initial ritual in person and I was told to touch each of the offerings in order to begin atoning for my sins and physically making penance. He said the particular goods necessary for my offering had been purchased and prepared in readiness; this was borne out by a large circular tray which was brought in and set down on the table.

The tray held three types of fruit, three types of flowers, an empty utensil (another pot in which I was to place nine grains), a dried coconut, some fennel and three sets of clothes still wrapped in their cellophane packaging – one male, one female and one child's – plus a pot for the donation of charity money that I was now to make.

The clothes, it seemed, were to represent the women and children I had so peremptorily abandoned, whilst the 'charity money' would total

1008 rupees (then £12 or $24) which was just about all I had on me at the time. I felt extraordinarily relieved at the surprisingly favorable size of my fine – and then just as extraordinarily humiliated by it only seconds later. The shame of it... Did it really mean that paltry sum was all that the four individuals I had so badly wronged deemed me to be worth, or had inflation been ignored? I didn't know, but it felt bad to have caught myself out by seeing it that way.

He then told me of the two Chapters covering my remedies, in particular the 13th and 14th *Kandams*. The 13th *Kandam* dealt with *"sins committed, and the remedial measures for getting rid of the effect of past birth's sins"* – which would now be accomplished by the following *puja*:

My donation of charity money (ie. the 1008 rupees I put in the cup); I was to bow to my palm-leaf within nine days of my reading (which I did that very afternoon); I was then to pray to my past-life leaf, together with the fruits, flowers, clothes and grains on the tray. On the ninth Thursday following my reading I was to light a lamp and pray in front of my God for penance, and then on the 48th Saturday after my reading I was to fast: I could only eat milk and fruits on that day, no salt or meat. Daily throughout the whole 192 days of my penance I was to 'feed the black crows', meditate for 15-20 minutes with my legs crossed and palms upwards in the correct yoga position (this was very difficult for me!), and give a prayer to my favorite God, and offer food or fruits to the animals or handicapped children. The Naadi holy men in Tamil Nadu were also to take over the chanting and praying on my behalf for the duration of my penance. (This turned out to be a very considerable undertaking for them).

It was odd about the 'black crows', animals and handicapped children. Where we had moved to in Wiltshire eight months previously (as my reading had so correctly noted) there is a large flock of crows resident in the trees all around us, as well as rather too many feral barnyard cats and kittens in the various outbuildings nearby on the land. Feeding all of them was therefore something that could be easily accomplished, but feeding the handicapped children not so easy. Unlike in India, there were none locally in the UK that we immediately knew of, so the reader told me I should feed the handicapped children we would see alongside the road on our way to Delhi airport instead (of which, sadly, there were far too many), and then continue to feed the cats and crows once back home – that would suffice.

So that's what we did, and I still do it. I have since learnt that there are many other forms my penance and *puja* could have taken, such as giving divine books on moral instruction to the poor, contributing money for a year's education for a student, supplying milk to a poor child for a year, aiding a poor widow or funding a poor couple's marriage, donating a cow to a poor person, feeding seven animals, making visits to 'my temple', donating money towards the building of a temple, or offering a statue of Shiva to a Shiva temple, to name a few.

As for the 14th *Kandam* – the "*wearing of a talisman* (a good luck charm) *for avoidance of enemies' troubles*" as well as the cleansing of '*others' jealousies*' and the health and other problems that I had had in my life so far. For all of that I had to do one more *puja,* comprising: chanting 1008 chants twice a day for the 192-day period (yes, it's that 1008 figure again), but thankfully the Brahmin priests in Tamil Nadu would sit and undertake this penance for me. I was to personally make four offerings, once every 48 days, and each time I should place ceremonial red and white ash on my forehead (the ash would be sent to me each time by the holy men, taken from the ash from the goods on my tray once they had been ceremonially burnt). I was to frame and display a copper plate (the talisman) that the Brahmin priests would make, prepare, bless and send to me after the 192 days of chanting had been completed; this would represent a visible and permanent sign of the true penance I had made and the ongoing good luck I would then have. On this plate the priests would write my name, date and place of birth and everything else to identify me and only me, to ensure all of their prayers – and mine – got to the right place!

Once all this had been done, provided I was sincere and carried out my parts to the letter, I could be assured that there would be much improvement in my life. He then lit the candles. They smoked sootily before settling down, intensifying the heat in the tiny room still more. Then, after another prayer and identifying me fully to Lord Shiva once again, he proceeded.

With beads of sweat starting on his brow, he rang the small bell and brought the tray towards me, proffering it for me to touch each item solemnly and then repeat the words and verses that he chanted, after which he hoisted it aloft and offered it to each of the gods in turn that lined the walls, ringing the bell to each one to call them, singing and chanting all the while. I then had to take the tray and stand and bow to each of them myself, working around the room and repeating his words to the many gods, then touch the ashen remains that already lay around the altar on the floor where my own offerings would be burnt. I touched them twice – once for the white ash, once for the red, both of which I had to place on my third eye, the spot on the forehead anointed by every Hindu.

Then it was over. With smiles and bows and thanks all round we adjourned to the corridor outside. It seemed that Angela, being already a much more blessed soul, need do no more *puja* than she had already done earlier that afternoon, so with my remedies now underway and our remaining time in India decidedly short, the time for settling the check had arrived.

All the work required of others on my behalf – my reading, the predictions and the remedies, the services of the reader and the Tamil holy men – was then itemized, costed out and set down together with the costs of the clothes and goods bought for my ceremonial *puja* plate. Including the charity money and the copper plate that I would in due course receive, the total came to something around 11,000 rupees (roughly $250 or £130).

From the way they looked nervously at me this clearly was no small sum to them (and to most ordinary Indians) yet for all that I had heard and learnt and was now assured I would be protected from and helped with, it seemed precious little to me.

I don't mean to sound arrogant or patronizing at all in saying that, but just think about doing 2016 chants each day for 192 days yourself, day in day out, at less than a fraction of a penny a time! And if my life really was mapped out and cleansed in this way and my health and fortune improved as I had been told it would, then their service was truly incredible in far more than its monetary value – I know of many back in the UK or USA who would spend as much on a meal out and think nothing of it.... so what on earth would they pay for the amazing proof I had received of who I was, along with the assurances I had been given of future happiness, health and success?

This sum now had to be found in rupees, which I did not have on me as I had not realized payment would have to be in cash in local currency. As a tourist I was hoping they would take Amex or Visa. There were also some costs arising from Angela's session. The whole lot came to just under 17,000 rupees (some £200 or $385). Dear Elias again came to our rescue until we had chance to recompense him once back at the hotel.

So it was finally done. All the necessary arrangements had been made and put in hand, and all we had to do now was fly home the following morning. It had been an extraordinary experience for us both, but far more so for me than for Angela, as it had left me completely uprooted and at sea in terms of faith, fate and feeling. The Naadis had quite simply blown me away with all they had said and done. What they offered had been the most intimate and personal expression of religion that I had ever come across or felt – it had been *my* reading, *my* leaf, *my* chart, *my* future, *my* life and lives, *my* past sins, *my* talisman and *my* penance.

It was all so utterly, strangely *intimate*. At each and every point it was down to me and my journey, and what I had (at some other time) decided to do with it. It was all very much a matter of faith, yes, but not one dressed up as any sort of religion that I could recognize. The Naadis may be Hindus but their practice is open to all creeds and religions and they pass no comments whatsoever on faith or creed other than the faith they have in the leaves they revere.

The remedies were delivered as promised. All of the instalments of red and white ash arrived (on time) in the UK for me throughout my penance, as did the little copper plate heralding the successful completion of my 192 days. This was a real little gem (see photo page 80). Nearly square, and measuring some 30mm x 40mm, or roughly one and a quarter inches by one and a half inches, it is wafer thin and beautifully and neatly etched with a tetrahedron, within which are the significant words and symbols relating to me all written in flowing Tamil script and dusted over in ash. It was exactly as they had said it would be, and from its varying hues and burnished tones it had clearly been subject to great heat as well. All in all, it is a unique and very unusual piece of work – now mounted in a suitably Indian frame as a piece of art to be treasured and pondered upon. It is a good and lasting friend and sits on my desk where I can see it in front of me every time I write.

There's another strange thing... I mentioned the tape-recording earlier, the record of the reader's words as spoken with Elias' translations, covering my predictions on one side and my remedies on the other. It runs to just under an hour and a half in total and while admittedly not all of it is spoken in perfect English, it is all readily understandable and easily followed.

Yet the oddest thing about it is that whenever I replay the tape – as I do from time to time, perhaps six or eight times in total by now – although the recorded words on it obviously do not and cannot change, their impact and meaning on me in places varies measurably each time. It's as if they are somehow new, or relate to me in a totally different way, so that I either hear something completely fresh and wholly relevant in the reading or the words have a quite different impact from the way I had heard and under-stood them before. It really is most odd. As fixed as the words are on the tape, they are still fluid enough to cover and answer whatever questions I have that have made me want to play the tape again. It has yet to disappoint; each time there's a new answer somehow, so the magic continues.

To me the whole Naadi experience has proved to be extraordinarily personal and compelling. So, fired by all I had experienced and learnt in such unassuming urban surroundings, I resolved to find out what more I could about the Naadis and their history.

CHAPTER FIVE

Andrew's Search: History Revealed

When I came away from India that first time, apart from everything else being suddenly upside down in my life, I found I was anxious to find out more of the story behind the leaves and how the process of storing the information of our lives upon them had come about. I will leave it to Angela to talk later on the spiritual aspects of the Naadis (being far better placed and qualified than I am to do so) but let me try to set down what I have managed to learn factually about the Naadis since I had my reading.

That is easier said than done. The history and background of the Naadis became ever more vague and elusive the further back I went. Not that I mean that in any sinister or pejorative way; in our several visits the Naadis have never been less than open and straightforward, helpful, honest, polite and modest: there has certainly been no intention to deceive or hoodwink as far as we have seen. It's just that it has been very hard to find out anything substantial about them that is factually definitive, consistent and documented well enough to be sure of, or that doesn't rely on apocryphal stories or assume you are content to accept it all just as it is told. Hence, the regrettable number of times you will read 'apparently' and 'it seems' and other illusory phrases in the text from here on – for which I can only apologize.

Like their faith in the leaves, the Naadis clearly rely on faith for much of their history, rooted as it is in ages old tradition. Everything you try to trace quickly diffuses back into the mists of time, leaving fable and handed-down reports and descriptions that are very likely to have been spun and embellished over the ages. The terms and words they use are also subject to many different spellings, which doesn't help the researcher.

Much is due to India's extremely strong oral tradition. Since time began knowledge was handed down by word of mouth from guru to student, elder-to-elder, generation upon generation. This may be one reason why I can find no Indian equivalent to Euclid or Archimedes, Pythagoras or Herodotus, for it simply wasn't done that way. Instead the knowledge was secretly and jealously guarded by the Rishis – the highest Brahmin priests – and only disseminated to the up-and-coming initiates that would follow them, thereby retaining all the latent power for themselves.

This began to change with the writing of the Hindu *Vedas,* the four Vedic texts covering creation, the universe and the gods, written around 1000 BC. These were followed by the *Upanishads,* the commentaries on the Vedas written circa 1000-300 BC dealing with the nature of deity and karma. These then were in turn followed by the *Epics,* the legends of the gods and humans (as with the *Mahabharata* and the *Bhagavad-Gita*) written between 200 BC and 200 AD, and it seems it was only through these great works that the printed word – and more importantly, the concepts and information behind them – became known to a wider populace. But even then it was largely only passed to the educated upper spheres of Indian society as it then was.

Whilst the period within which these were all written covers an impressive span of time – some 1,200 years – it is still nothing like the period between 200 AD and the time of good old Sri Kausika (the Rishi responsible for my reading) and his mentor, Lord Shiva, which had supposedly taken place somewhere between 2,000 and 4,000 years earlier. That's the sort of historical jump that is a leap of faith I tend to have trouble with.

* * *

Talking of leaps of faith, I came across a story by Sant Sri Asaramji Ashram that I rather liked. It tells of a certain Lieutenant Colonel Martin who, in 1879, was leading elements of the British Army in the war against Afghanistan. (So what else is new?)

It seems that whenever he was away at the front, Colonel Martin regularly sent mail back home to his wife in Agar Malva to reassure her he was alive and well. All very proper and correct, just as I would have imagined an upright British colonial officer to have acted in those times.

To her great dismay, however, his messages stopped. Later, while she was out riding, she came across the temple of Baijnath Mahadev and was drawn by the mantras she could hear being sung and the instruments she could hear being played inside. She went in and found out that the Brahmin priests were worshipping Lord Shiva. Seeing how miserable she was, they stopped and asked her what was wrong, so she told them. They said that Lord Shiva always listened to the prayers of those who worshipped him and he could help her if she wished, whereupon she began to learn and sing a mantra that lasted for 11 days, and left promising to renovate the temple if her husband returned home safely.

On the eleventh day, the last day of the mantra, she received a message. Her husband had written: "*I was regularly sending messages to you from the battlegrounds but suddenly the Pathans surrounded us on all sides. We were trapped in a situation where there was no chance of escape. Suddenly I saw an Indian Yogi with long hair wearing a lion skin and carrying a weapon with three points, like a trident. Seeing this great man, the Pathans started running back, and with his appearance our bad situation turned to one of victory. That great Yogi told me that he had come to rescue me because he was very pleased with my wife's prayers.*"

Lady Martin promptly re-visited the temple and fell at the foot of Lord Shiva's statue and wept, for the yogi her husband reported seeing was dressed and armed exactly as Lord Shiva is depicted.

A few weeks later, her husband returned and she narrated the whole incident to him. She and he both became devotees of Lord Shiva and in 1883 they donated 15,000 rupees (a massive sum at the time) to renovate the temple. This is recorded on a stone plaque that is still at the temple site today, celebrating it as the only Hindu temple ever to be built by 'Britishers'.

* * *

It is worse still should you decide to look up 'Naadi' on the web, where seemingly more and more sites appear online every day, each with a token amount of background information dressed up (sometimes rather misleadingly) as Naadi 'history' yet presented in ways to suit the particular aims of the site.

It is a subject that is obviously becoming ever more popular and as such is falling prey to money-seeking opportunists who will happily trade on the 'Naadi' name by promising readings covering everything to everyone. In theory this means there is no need for you to leave your doorstep to meet with them as we did, as you can have your thumbprint analyzed by any number of supposed Naadi practitioners back in India via the internet if you are prepared to risk it and pay them what they want up front.

Yet how you would then know and trust the validity of what you are being told, or where that information truly comes from, whether the leaf you are told of is yours and not someone else's or indeed whether it exists at all – I frankly don't know. Having witnessed some true Naadis at work, it seems to me to be of vital importance that someone you trust and who knows you extremely well is there on hand to answer every one of the very many subtle and intimate questions that need to be answered before your leaf can be properly and finally determined. Anything less carries great risk, and it can only be the very greatest risk if you are not even there at all, however much detail you think you may have supplied them about you when mailing them your thumbprint. Then again, sending them all that information beforehand completely defeats the point – it is they who should be telling you all of that, not vice versa, for that way any fool can 'confirm' what you've already told them and then make a few random predictions for the years ahead.

That is not at all what the sincere Naadis are all about, so I for one would not recommend you trust anything less than undergoing the whole experience yourself, in person, with a Naadi reader who has been personally vouched for and comes highly recommended.

Nor do I believe you can do it properly for yourself, although you can now buy CDs over the internet that supposedly give you all the means and answers. Well, take it from me, having purchased several books on Naadi astrology (see a later Chapter) it really isn't that easy and you will need a wealth (if not a lifetime) of new knowledge and a great deal of hard experience to even make a start with it.

The true Naadi philosophy is very much the province of initiates only, as the knowledge is passed on to those who are already aware of it or are destined to become so, and only a very small number of readers can faithfully and accurately read and interpret the poetic Tamil, Teluga or other inscriptions on the smooth, smoke-treated leaves with the depth of knowledge and integrity that is truly required.

* * *

But could I at least determine or check just how old the palm-leaves were in our bundles? It seemed the obvious thing to start with. The writings were supposed to be thousands of years old, but how long would the leaves survive before they perished? Was the writing on them as old, or older? So just how far back could one reliably trace the words, or test their use as a means of recording knowledge that had previously been handed down by word of mouth?

Well, ancient writing came in many forms – on cave walls, stone slabs, animal skins, birch bark, copper scrolls, clay blocks, papyrus; but using palm leaves was a wholly new one on me when we first went to India. When I first heard of it I thought I had simply misunderstood what had been said and that it was really just another form of 'palmistry'. With hindsight this was partly right I suppose (given that the markings on your thumb – at least – were critical for your identification), yet clearly it was wrong at the same time.

To my ignorance I find that palm leaves were a natural writing medium for a very significant chunk of the world for many centuries from antiquity until well into the 19th Century. This turned out to be the case for the whole South East Asian region, not only India and Sri Lanka but Malaysia, Burma, Thailand, Laos, Nepal, Cambodia and Indonesia as well, where each country had developed and used the palm's leaves to reflect their own particular writing styles, methods of preparation, painting and decoration techniques and to establish their cultural identities. Each of those countries now has its own reference libraries and prized collections of ancient palm leaves to preserve and boast about.

Yet how were palm leaves used, practically? I had imagined palm leaves to be long, spiky things that would hardly lend themselves to writing, let alone survive intact for many centuries as some were supposed to have done.

Palms are indeed old – the date palm was cultivated by the Mesopotamians and other Middle Eastern races as long as 5,000 years ago, so that certainly fitted the bill. Palm trees are also very prevalent – there are some 2600 species worldwide, found in habitats as wide-ranging as rainforest and desert, and because of their remarkable usefulness economically, they have played an important part in the historical development of those civilizations that naturally grew up with them.

I was also surprised to learn that nearly every part of the palm has been used in some form or other to provide indigenous peoples with most of their basic needs, from simple shade and shelter to thatching and all of the fundamental building materials they might require, as well as ropes, furniture, clothing, cooking oils, nets, medicines, foods, drinks and many other staple products needed to maintain their lives and their livelihoods. And very importantly, as it was a natural, fast-growing and widespread resource, it was cheap too.

So useful was it in fact that in some cultures the palm even became a symbol of peace, fertility and victory, particularly in pre-Christian times when it was obviously seen as being important enough to warrant mention in both the Bible and the Koran. So maybe it is not so unnatural that the populous and ever-useful palm became a surface for writing on as well. Yet how was it done?

Two kinds were found to be the most appropriate for writing – the strong *Palmyra*, which needed a relatively dry climate, and the softer, more flexible *Talibot*, which thrived in a wetter coastal climate. The thick leaves of the *Palmyra* were prone to insect attack, however, and so were used for writing letters and notes, whilst the less insect-prone but thinner-leaved *Talibot* was more suitable for documenting the more important treatises and books – which all seems somewhat odd when you find out it is the *Talibot* palm that also provides all of the fans, mats, basket ware, wicker trays, umbrellas and other handicrafts used today for the tourist and domestic trades.

In order to make them suitable for writing, the leaves first had to be properly prepared. This process varied regionally, but the width of the leaves was fairly constant whichever area they were in – somewhere between 50-90mm – naturally determining the size and format of the pages they could make. In instances where larger manuscripts were required, the leaves would be stitched together along one edge with a needle and thread to make the pages wider.

The leaves were then treated; I have found references to their being interlaid with paw paw, papaya nuts and pineapple leaves, and rolled and boiled in vats until they were fully pliant, after which they were rinsed in clean water and dried in the open air with a little sun before polishing. This was done by rubbing the leaf with a stone over a certain wood (*Alstonia Scholaries* apparently) until smooth, whereupon two holes were punched into each one and a cord strung through, thereby slowly but surely making up the bundles of leaves that we were to see in due course.

It then only remained to ensure they were all the same size and protected against insect attack, which was done by pressing hard down on the stacks of leaves and cutting them uniformly all round, then burning the raw edges and the perimeters of the two holes with a hot implement before finally putting them inside a wooden mould to be sealed airtight all round. The bundles so formed were then held in storage, ready for use.

Each bundle can be likened to a book, with the pages held between the two hardwood panels as covers, each roughly the size of an old imperial foot rule but much thicker, and the whole thing bound together by cording through the two punched holes in the center and wrapped around the outside. Depending on the value and significance that the book would have, the covers could then be enhanced or substituted with ivory or ebony and even embossed with silver or gold, precious or semi-precious stones, lacquer work or mother-of-pearl, with each one worked to whatever particular design or pattern the author or client required.

This was not necessary as far as our own Naadi bundles were concerned, where each leaf or *'ola'* (see photo page 20) had been etched on by a monk or scribe in *vatta ezhuthu* – the Tamil script – with all of the letters formed the same size and evenly spaced, without gaps or punctuation, by means of a sharp stylus called an *ezhuthani*. Other languages were also used depending upon the region – Telugu, Pali, Singhalese, Sanskrit and even English during the time of the colonial regime.

Great care was needed to avoid the stylus splitting the leaf, so each leaf had to be rested on the palm of the hand so that the correct writing pressure could be gauged, then the letters were carefully inscribed from left to right with the other hand using the thumb to guide the stylus along the leaf's veins, which, being generally straight, served as marker lines.

The ink was also special. Colorless when written, it obviously could not be easily read, so the writing was wiped with lamp-black or soot to increase its legibility. Thereafter the leaves were kept flexible and protected from their many natural enemies – light, climatic changes, staining, discoloration, insect and fungal attack – which was generally accomplished by regularly rubbing them with soft cotton soaked in peacock oil. This still is done on 'auspicious' occasions and certainly no less frequently than every two or three years.

But the question still remained. Even with thorough, regular rubbings of peacock oil, how old could some of the leaves be?

To date I have found no evidence of Indian manuscripts surviving from a time before the 10th Century, ie. 1000 AD. However, there is a reference to Chinese records that indicates that the palm-leaf system was in use in India in the second Century AD – a fragment of text from an Indian drama having been found dating from that time. Yet this form of writing had already been recorded in Sri Lanka a century earlier, circa 100 AD, and by the fifth Century it appears to have been in common use throughout the whole South-East Asia region. So it seems quite possible that we could be talking as far back as the time when Christ walked the earth 2,000 years ago. The palm leaf system continued to be used even after the introduction of paper by the Dutch in the early 1600s and the printing-press in the 19th Century, and it still remained in common practice in the more remote areas where important legal documents (wills, land registry titles etc) were most often inscribed on leaves through choice, as evidenced by many British colonials then trading in the region.

Even today it seems that the palm leaf is still the preferred medium for certain Hindu religious texts. Nevertheless, with the new techniques and materials for writing that had emerged by the 19th Century, the maintenance of the numerous bundles and even more numerous leaves, and the skills of those that knew how to prepare, write and maintain them, became the province of a progressively smaller and more esoteric number.

While it was clear to me after doing some research that the system had been in use for many centuries, it did not necessarily mean that the leaves themselves were that old, for it was also clear that throughout the period it was standard practice for any leaves that had become too discolored or had deteriorated too far to be copied afresh onto new leaves, then substituted back into the bundles. It is well recorded that the Kings of Tanjore gave instructions between the 9th and 13th Centuries AD that any and all leaves found to be fading or beginning to disintegrate were to be completely and precisely re-written on fresh leaves, all of which was to be carried out by scholars specifically appointed by them to do so. By then such necessary replenishment had become a tradition that was faithfully maintained by all subsequent dynasties and people interested in the leaves, such as the Maratha king Sarabhoji and the great Chola kings, who in turn had translations made into Telugu (another southern Indian language).

So while you sit there having your Naadi reading, the leaves you see before you may not be as old as you'd like to imagine, or indeed particularly old at all – certainly not nearly as old as the words of the text that is written upon them. By such means each leaf could be either a relatively new copy of a copy of a copy, or a very well-preserved older leaf that has survived from a much earlier time. Three hundred to four hundred years is the longest any single leaf can be expected to remain intact without needing to be replaced.

Yet however old the leaf is, the wording of the text upon it will still be just as the wording on that very first leaf, with every mark and syllable exactly as it was spoken by Lord Shiva to whichever of the *Sapta Rishis* whose predictions you are listening to now.

And the age of that original wording? I have yet to run it to ground in any way that I could hand-on-heart say convinces me that they are the three, four or five thousand years old they are supposed to be.

Sample of writing etched on each leaf

* * *

But it is not just the significant details of your or my life and past and present lives that is contained on these leaves, far from it. Personal histories are one small category of the knowledge that was laid down and kept in this way.

There are two classical languages in India: Tamil and Sanskrit. The treatises in the Tamil language alone cover an extraordinarily impressive number of subjects – Ayurvedic medicine, anatomy, astronomy, astrology, acupuncture, agriculture, animal husbandry and veterinary science, architecture, carpentry, drama, love songs, martial arts, mathematics, music, metalworking, poetry, recipes, sculpture, ship-building, temple art and architecture, writing techniques and yoga – in other words all aspects of the Tamil literature, art, language and culture known at that time, which was very considerable.

For at least the last two thousand years, once India's oral tradition was finally broken, the monks and scribes had recorded much of India's scientific, literary and cultural heritage on palm leaves. Upwards of 100,000 of these apparently still remain unread, untranslated or unpublished – a figure that is believed to represent ten per cent of the leaves still in existence, and therefore only a small proportion of the total knowledge that the Indian and Tamil civilizations hold. To me it sounds a bit like the rainforest, where goodness knows how many medicinal and other benefits remain unknown, untapped and likely to be lost forever as the ongoing lack of awareness continues and their destruction increases year by year.

Not that this is likely to happen with the palm leaf treatises, thankfully, for there is much work currently going on in India, Asia and elsewhere to locate, purchase, preserve, photograph and copy – chemically, digitally and otherwise – the as-yet unread leaves for reference and publication at some future time. So who knows what new medical treatments might arise when the ancient uses of the traditional Asian herbs and minerals have finally been uncovered and disclosed?

* * *

Surprising to learn as all this was, it was still not getting me any closer to the Naadis, who seemingly have little interest in the major treatises (apart perhaps from astrology) or any of the leaves other than those that have to do with their work, in other words, those dealing with people's past and future lives.

Tradition would seem to bear this out, for tradition has it that the Naadi readers acted as court astrologers at least as far back as 500 AD. This makes sense to me as it would ensure their survival through the patronage they would have received, while allowing the precious leaf collections to be guarded and carefully retained by the families that held them – much like a monopoly or closed shop – handing them on to their sons and heirs who had been trained and schooled to continue in the ancient, esoteric craft down through the generations.

In this way it seems the town of Vaitheeswarankoil, near Chidabaram, became the main center for palm-leaves in Tamil Nadu, as it still is today, and this is the place where Lord Shiva is said to have once assumed the role of a doctor, or *Vaidhya,* to alleviate the sufferings of his many followers. It was this community, along with the Valluvars (another center in Tamil Nadu specializing in astrology), that made further copies during the 13th Century, all of which have been handed down, enabling them to make their livelihoods through predictive astrology.

Later, under British colonial rule in the 1700s, the many other leaf collections that the occupiers had access to but did not want (principally the collections dealing with any subject other than herbal cures, medicines, science and alchemy) were arbitrarily auctioned and sold off to anyone who was still interested in them. Many were bought up by the Vaitheeswarankoil and Valluvar families to supplement their own collec-tions, but sadly it seems many others were cherry-picked and broken up to suit individual wants and needs.

All of which may perhaps explain why, until the 1930s, the Naadis were largely unknown to most Hindu astrologers and just about everyone else in or outside of India. Even then, those that were aware of them were apparently either quick to dismiss them as being useless, or failed to bother to comprehend their potential value. As a result, many leaves were left to rot in private collections or were lost, dispersed far and wide over the country. Only comparatively recently has their worth been recognized enough for them to be sought out and recovered by the major Indian libraries – those in Chennai, Tanjore and Madras – which appreciate their historic and astrological importance and purchase them whenever and wherever they become available. But whether it is because the great collections were dispersed or whether it is because spiritually, as the Naadis believe, not everyone is ready to find their leaf, it is said that only some 40 per cent or so of the world's population is now likely to be 'found'.

Yet amazingly, access to the Naadis applies to whatever corner of the world you are living in or come from. There is no veto or embargo. As we and other westerners have demonstrated, the leaves are not only for the Indian people but for foreigners too, from whatever religion, faith or none. The Naadis do not discriminate and do not ask you your faith, they are merely certain of one thing – whoever is destined to come to meet their leaf will come, for *whoever wishes to look into the leaves will go to them on their own accord.*

* * *

The word '*Naadi*' has at least seven different meanings:
1. In the Tamil language '*Naadi*' means '*in pursuit of*' or '*in search of*.
2. '*Naadi*' also means '*those who are destined to come on their own accord*'.

Angela and I had no problem with either of these meanings as we had gone forward, being very much 'in pursuit of' our palm-leaves. Then when they had been found, we felt certain we had been 'destined to come of our own accord' to meet them, particularly given the chance way we had heard about them in the first place, and then again when we heard that it was written on both our leaves that we would come to meet them exactly when we did, the only time we could ever do so.

3. 'Naadi' are the pulses used in the Ayurvedic medicine system to determine which disease a patient has and what strength it is by means of pulses that throb under the skin of the wrist, as with acupuncture. Both systems were covered in the palm leaf Treatises.

4. 'Naadi' also means 'swara' or 'breath movement'. A human being inhales and exhales on average around 21,600 times every day. The yogis state that this is the basis of all things.

Every human being has two nostrils which in Naadi terms are classified as yidakalai (the Moon, which represents breathing through the left nostril) and pinkalai (the Sun, which represents breathing through the right nostril). There is also a third way, called sulimunkalai, which is breathing (you guessed it) through both nostrils at once. It is said that the great Sages, those like the Septa Rishis who had acquired the eight great mystic powers, used this third form of breathing to gain their knowledge of the Past, Present and Future, and through the spiritual power that resulted they were able to access the good and bad deeds of all who came before them seeking help. When coupled with the 'secrets' that the nine planets could disclose, this would enable clear explanations to be given to all who sought them.

Yet the Naadi astrologer giving out these details has to be of impec-cable and unimpeachable character himself as well, someone whose soul carries only good deeds from past lives, and is of a totally 'charitable and compassionate disposition'. That way his predictions could be nothing less than genuine and true, which may of course be one reason why there are so few of them.

5. *'Naadi'*, when used in *'Naadi Shastra'* relates to energy-channel studies, which are descriptions of patterns of data that are then recorded.

6. *'Naadi'*, as in *'Naadi Kuta'*, is used for testing compatibility and for matching and making marriage alliances. This brings me back to the readings we had both had; compatibility in marriage is one of the subjects the *Kandams* cover. Indeed one of our Delhi guides had been married by just such means, as had his sons and daughters after him, and as far as he was concerned there was no other way to do it.

7. *'Naadi'* in astrology is a small unit of an arc of the zodiac (and therefore its corresponding time) ranging from $1/150^{th}$ to $1/600^{th}$ of a sign – ie. from 12 minutes to 3 minutes of arc. Any true Naadi is based on the 360 degrees of the zodiac divided into the 12 signs, or *Rashis,* with 1800 sub-sections for each one – ie. 12 x 1800 or 21,600 in total (strangely the same figure as for the 'breaths' above) based on the 24 hours in every day. So there is seemingly one individual destiny every four seconds.

Highly intriguing I thought. Hence my next chapter.

CHAPTER SIX

It's All Written In Your Stars: Naadi Astrology
Andrew:

In Naadi astrological terms, people born with a particular segment of arc as their Ascendant are deemed to be subject to very definite life patterns, with the explanations of those patterns expressed in terms of planetary movement. It is these interpretations that are then used in conjunction with – and to supplement – the staggeringly precise details of each of the lives recorded on the palm-leaves.

This was particularly interesting to me given that the Naadi reader checked both of our birth-times before preparing our predictions, and so I determined to find out more about Naadi astrology. I read somewhere that "researching Naadi astrology is a Herculean task... it is just like authoring an encyclopaedia" and from what I've been able to find out to date, I'm very happy to underscore that statement. So bear with me.

There are many ancient Naadi astrological texts apparently still in existence, some of which are concerned purely with astrological matters while others also link to palmistry. Either way, astrology figures prominently in the Naadi system and had great sway and relevance in the interpretation of our own readings once we had been identified.

'*Jyotisha*' is the Hindu system of astrology and is regarded as one of the oldest independent schools dealing with it, and one that has affected all other such schools in India. Historically it is very ancient and very much a part of the holistic approach to life and spirituality that the Hindus revere and practice. It is also a fundamental part of the *Vedas*, the earliest treatises written in the Indian language that was mentioned earlier, other aspects of which cover mathematics, architecture, medicine and alchemy.

It is well known that Hindus believe 'karma' determines the fortune (and indeed misfortune) of every human being, and in jyotish astrology it is the '*grahas*' – the planets – that influence every moment of our lives, decisions and actions. The Hindus look to the planets to forewarn, influence and mitigate whatever bad karma is on its way. In ancient times this specialist astrological knowledge would have been the sole province of the Brahmins (the Indian priests of the very highest caste), but more recently it has become commonplace for other Hindus and western astrologers to practice it as well, even if some westerners fail to see it as a true 'science'.

In Hindu culture, newborn children are traditionally named based upon their jyotish charts. This was made very clear to us when speaking with others who were waiting in the Naadis' reception area in Delhi. Our tourist guide and courier, a man in his early forties, told us that each of his five children's names had been determined by the date they were born, as was his own name, his wife's name, his father's and mother's names and so on for generations back. Any decisions he had to make in organizing his life, his business, his household – such as buying a car, moving house – were made by this method of timing, as these events, to his mind, were all totally dependant upon the date and the arrangement of the heavens at the time for their outcome, which was why he was consulting the Naadis when we met him. For him there was simply no other way to do it.

For this reason, they will visit the Naadis whenever they want to hear one, two or more of the *Kandams,* dealing with whatever subject should happen to be on their mind at the time, be it their mother's health, an upcoming business meeting, the purchase of a new house, the best time to try for the next child, the likely outcome of a relative's operation and so on.

Nevertheless, I have read somewhere that generally, regarding future predictions, the Naadis' accuracy only averages between 30 per cent and 55 per cent. I can only say that all of my predictions that were supposed to have happened in the period since my reading have in fact done so (as indeed have Angela's), although obviously neither of us can speak of those that lie still ahead.

About this the Naadis have one comment to make. They say that clients who come to them with a sincere frame of mind will fare much better than those who do not. So if you're cynical or sceptical, beware – even if I have to admit that I was more than a little that way myself before all of this. Perhaps my sudden change of heart when confronted with so much stunning accuracy made all the difference, who can say?

* * *

There are three main branches to Hindu / Vedic astrology – *Siddhanta* (the application of astronomy), *Samhita* (the prediction of important events such as wars between countries, earthquakes, omens, portents, financial matters) and *Hora* (predictive astrology).

There are then further sub-branches – some 18 or 20 of them – which deal with horoscopes, predictions based on names or sounds, the determination of the optimum times to do something or gain most benefit from it, numerology and many others such as palmistry, foot readings (using the lines on the soles of the feet), the interpretation of dreams, omens and portents, phrenology (reading the bumps of the head), physiognomy and marks or moles on the body... all manner of methods are used, within which Naadi astrology is classified as 'an ancient treatise having detailed predictions for individuals.'

When comparing Hindu and western astrology, the principal difference appears to be the method used to measure the zodiac. The Hindu or Vedic system uses the sidereal zodiac (where the position of the stars is fixed, against which the motion of the planets is measured) whilst the western system relies more on the tropical zodiac (where the planets' motion is measured against the Sun's position at the time of the Spring Equinox). The difference between them seemingly only becomes noticeable after many centuries as a result of the precession of equinoxes that have taken place.

Both systems are ancient, but the Vedic system has further subsystems that allow for predictions and their interpretation using methods and elements not found elsewhere, whereby auspicious times of day or dates of the month can be determined, together with the mathematical analysis of a human's lifetime into periods which depend on the location of the Moon in a particular constellation at the time of his or her birth.

This made sense – the second page of the Naadi booklet prepared and given to me by my Naadi reader sets out the position of the Moon and other planets on my chart, giving their location at the precise time of my birth, which my Naadi reader then used to calculate my future predictions and remedies.

The *grahas* or planets also include the lunar nodes (*Rahu* and *Ketu*) but because of the age of the Vedic system, do not include the more recently discovered planets Neptune, Uranus and (dare I mention it now?) Pluto. Only the seven classical planets and the Moon nodes are involved in Vedic astrology, each having an abbreviated Sanskrit name to match the English name and each representing certain aspects of life:

Name	Sanskrit Abb / Name	Representing
Sun	*Sy or Su / Surya*	*the Soul of all*
Moon	*Ch or Mo / Chandra*	*the Mind*
Mars	*Ma / Mangala or Kuj*	*Confidence, Strength*
Mercury	*Bu or Me / Budha*	*Speech, Communication*
Jupiter	*Gu or Ju / Guru*	*Knowledge and Happiness*
Venus	*Sk or Ve / Sukra*	*Wealth, Pleasure, Potency*
Saturn	*Sa / Sani*	*Grief, Career, Longevity*
Ascending Lunar	*Rahu*	*Force creating chaos in life*
Descending Lunar	*Ketu*	*Supernatural influences*

In the photograph of my own chart (see page 74) you will note the 12 Houses grouped around the centre square marked 'RASI' or *Rashi*, representing the zodiac. Most of us are aware of the signs of Aries, Taurus, Gemini, Cancer, Leo, Virgo, Libra, Scorpio, Capricorn, Sagittarius,

Aquarius and Pisces, and their 12 corresponding Houses. These Houses in turn signify the Head, Face, Arms, Heart, Stomach, Hip, Groin, Genitals, Thighs, Knees, Ankles and Feet of the human body. Aries, Gemini, Leo, Libra, Sagittarius and Aquarius are all deemed to be male signs (and as such are considered 'malefic' or cruel), whilst Taurus, Cancer, Virgo, Scorpio, Capricorn and Pisces are all female signs (and so considered beneficial or soft).

The 12 Houses relate to the 12 basic *Kandams*, so the Second House is to do with Wealth, Family, Education; the Fourth House is to do with Mother, Home, Vehicles, Property... it all ties together very neatly. It gets progressively more complicated, which is where the years of study and experience come in and why there is no way I could ever hope to hang a 'Naadi Astrologer' sign outside my door.

We bought numerous books on Naadi astrology whilst we were in India, in the vain hope that they would give us a more detailed explanation of how it all works. Sure the knowledge is all there, somehow, but in such endlessly subtle, complex and voluminous ways that you cannot hope to achieve more than the most basic appreciation – not even an understanding – unless you are prepared to study it in very great depth over a period of many years. If you were to pick up a book which sets out the thousand upon thousand of horoscopes detailing every individual nuance and meaning that the planets, stars, the Moon and other influences can have in whatever myriad different ways they can be arranged in, you'll begin to see what I mean. Small wonder then that the true Naadi practitioners are very few and far between and do not take their art (or is it science?) lightly.

To further complicate matters, in northern India the layout of the chart differs slightly even if the House positions remain fixed. The First House is always in the top left-hand corner with the rest following on round counter-clockwise and is indicated by numbers on the chart. In southern India and Tamil Nadu where our Naadis come from, the signs also have fixed positions (Aries is always in the same place) but the First House is in the square *below* the top left-hand corner – the Ascendant square – with the rest then moving round *clockwise*. Vedic astrology involves a complex reading of displacement of the planets from their natural homes in specific Houses, and to the Naadi astrologer the Ascendant is the start of everything he works from.

Using the countless number of potential horoscopes that have been written down since time immemorial to cover every possible planetary arrangement and influence, the Naadi astrologer can prepare your predic-

---

SRI KAUSIKA MAHASIVA NADI JOTHIDA NILAYAM
E-1/209, Second Floor, Near Krishna Market,
Lajpat Nagar-I, New Delhi- 110024

Ph. : 29817280, 29813679

NAME : MR. ANDREW

Ravi, Rahu	Bud	–	–
Guru Suk	RASI		–
			Man Sani
Moon	–		Keth

Year : virothi
Month : pankuni
Date (Tamil) : 26
Day : Saturday
Star : pooraadam
Rasi : thanu
Lagan : Makara
English Date of Birth : 8/4/50

Extract from Andrew's Booklet

tions and remedies for you in a matter of minutes or hours, based on what he has found.

If you look at my chart, you will see that Jupiter and Venus are both in the First House, the Ascending Lunar Node is in the Second, Mercury is at home in the Third House, Mars and Saturn are in the Seventh House, the Descending Lunar Node is in the Eighth House and the Moon is in the Tenth House. The Ascendant or *Lagan* is the most important and influential sign – this is the sign rising on the eastern horizon at the time of one's birth – in my case this is Capricorn, or *Makara* in Sanskrit as noted on the table below the chart. The *Janma Rashi* is the sign in which the Moon was placed at birth.

As to the pages that follow in my Naadi booklet these are unlikely to be readily or usefully understandable to most western eyes, even though they may comprise the exact words, verses and phrases used for me in my reading, as they are all written in Tamil or Telugu.

Quite by chance we tested this when we went back to see the Naadi readers last year, when I asked for an updated reading to cover my current year in greater depth. The Naadi reader called for my Naadi booklet so that he could refer to the original text, and then repeated virtually everything I had been told before. Disappointingly he added nothing new except to say that in the intervening period 'I had found my God', something I was surprised to find on reflection to feel strangely very right and true.

* * *

I am not expert enough to take you into the science of *jyotish*, any more than I could any other form of astrology. But many contemporary Indian scientists have criticised the Indian universities for introducing Vedic astrology into the curriculum, seeing it as anything but a scientific discipline. They have stated their dissent:

"We the members of the Indian scientific community feel that the proposal by the UGC to introduce Vedic Astrology (Jyotir Vigyan) and Vastushastra in Indian universities is a giant leap backwards, undermining whatever scientific credibility our country may have so far achieved. We request the UGC to abandon this ill judged course of action." [R Ramachandran. 'Degrees In Pseudo-Science'. People's Democracy.]

However, to offset such dismissive criticism I would quote the following endorsements I have come across in defence of the Vedas and the Vedic systems or *Vedanta:*

Alfred North Whitehead, the celebrated English mathematician, philosopher and logician, stated that the *"Vedanta is the most impressive metaphysics the human mind has conceived."*

Lin Yutang, the Chinese scholar and author wrote, *"India was China's teacher in trigonometry, quadratic equations, grammar, phonetics…"*

Carl Sagan, one of the most renowned scientists of the 20th Century, said, *"Vedic Cosmology is the only one in which the time scales correspond to those of modern scientific cosmology."*

Nobel Laureate Count Maeterlinck wrote that Vedic Astrology was *"a Cosmology which no European conception has ever surpassed."*

French astronomer Jean-Claude Bailly checked and corroborated the accuracy and age of Vedic astronomical instruments and measurements and found them *"more ancient than those of the Greeks or Egyptians"*, adding that *"the movements of the stars calculated 4,500 years ago does not differ by a minute from the tables of today."*

So not everyone places such poor judgment on its value for education!

Taking a simple overview, bear in mind that Vedic literature contains the details and descriptions of some very advanced scientific methods and techniques, many of which cannot be bettered or reproduced even with the technological reach we have today. For example, modern metallurgists have been unable to make iron of comparable quality to the 22 ft high iron pillar that still stands in the open air in New Delhi, yet it was forged – all done by hand – sometime in the third Century BC. Weighing six tons, for over 2000 years it has not rusted nor even been damaged or destroyed by gunfire, having been hit by an artillery shell during the Sacking of Delhi in 1737.

Equally impressive is the 90 ft tall astronomical instrument built in stone and known as the *Samrat Yantra*, commissioned by the great Moghul King Suwai Jai Singh in 1727, that still stands in Jaipur today; it continues to measure time to an accuracy of less than two seconds per day.

In mathematics, the expertise and knowledge first documented in the ancient palm leaf treatises is unsurpassed. I mentioned earlier that I'd found no Indian equivalent to Euclid or Pythagoras, yet Pythagoras himself went to India to learn all about geometry – the theorem that now bears his name had already been found and written down in the Vedic *Shatapatha Brahmana* as well as the *Sulba Sutra* centuries before he was born, while algebra and the decimal system (based on the power of ten with any remainder being carried over to the next column) had – like the concept of infinity – already been expounded and set down in the *Taittriya Samhita*.

The binary system, comparatively recently found so essential for computers, is the same meter system that the Vedic verses were written in. For this reason NASA have become so interested in it today in developing techniques to pioneer and realise the next steps to Artificial Intelligence.

And so the list goes on. Cosmetic surgery including rhinoplasty was regularly practised by Indian surgeons in the 17th Century. Hashing techniques similar to those used by contemporary search engines such as Google were already used in Vedic musicology. Sounds the Indian mantras used have been found to have extraordinary subtle and powerful effects, and were mentioned in the Vedas as being used as weapons as well as for more peaceful pursuits such as meditation and spiritual purposes.

The point I am trying to make is that while the Brahmans' ancient oral traditions may have left us with little record of the great discoveries and progress their civilization and culture had made until the *Vedas* were first published some 3,000 years ago, it certainly does not mean that the knowledge was not there beforehand, and had not been there for many hundreds if not thousands of years before that. The very earliest universities were founded in India, and Hermes, or 'Trismegistrus', the great Egyptian sage who lived circa 3,000 years BC, left writings and records that are now some 5,000 years old, which is just about the time the Naadis expect us westerners to believe that Lord Shiva spoke to the *Sapta Rishis* when they documented all he told them onto the palm leaves.

This knowledge included the details of our own lives. So with all that the great Indian Sages clearly knew and gave to the other races and countless individuals that followed them down the centuries, who am I to argue against that possibility?

* * *

Let me go back to the Indian guide and courier. I mentioned earlier that he, his wife and all of his family had had their names determined by the dates on which they were born. Another aspect of Naadi astrology is based upon the fundamental importance of your given name.

To the Naadis, your name alone warrants a great deal of analysis, having within it both 'good' and 'bad' aspects. While they believe your destiny will be determined by the dominance and position of the various planets at the time of your birth, if destiny favors you then you will in turn adopt a very powerful name, thereby enhancing your good fortune and assuring yourself even more of a happy and contented life. It follows that the opposite is also true– a weak or powerless name will only encourage misery and suffering.

Each name is made up of individual letters, forming an overall sound when the complete name is spoken. To the Naadis, each individual letter is overtly governed by a specific planet or celestial, and that sound is covertly governed by a magical, hidden power, with the complete name having an overall overt sound and overall covert magical hidden power which is in turn governed by two holy planets.

So the realization of a name that will maximize the overt and covert powers within it is what the Naadis seek to achieve, with the two divine forces combining to determine the strength and depth of life and liveliness that the name then holds.

In this way, every name has two elements – an outer and an inner. The outer, called the 'body', is the natural sound of the name made up of the natural sound of the letters, whilst the inner, called the 'soul', is the magic of the 'holy sounds' within it. If both elements are working in a happy harmony, then the owner of the name will lead a very happy and prosperous life indeed.

Using the *Rasi* or Moon sign, the horoscope then comes into play, the Moon acting as the 'body' and the *Lagna,* the Ascendant, acting as the 'soul', both of which are studied very closely by the Naadis as they determine which holy planets are involved.

So goes the thinking, and I began to see why names had such importance to our tourist guide. Thinking about it further, perhaps it's not so unusual after all. We all enjoy nice sounds – they can delight as well as inspire, amuse as well as intrigue, whilst harsher, heavier sounds can kill a mood or destroy enjoyment.

To the Naadis, all this is quite obvious – to them 'divine' sounds will naturally imbue natural power to all the living and non-living things around them. So it is perfectly natural that a name will inspire friendship or enmity, peace or hostility. But it goes a little further too. The Naadis say that the 'natural' sound of the letters (the 'body') can only be heard on earth, whilst the 'divine' or 'holy' sound (the 'soul') will be heard on 'all of the fourteen worlds'. The fourteen worlds was a new one on me until Angela explained it represents the seven worlds above our physical plane and the seven below.

The 'holy' sound in a name in turn affects three classes of celestials –

the 'syllable-celestials', the 'higher syllable-celestials' and the 'supreme celestials', who govern the heavens and decide the good and evil that we experience. It is beyond mere humans to hear the 'holy' sound. So, by analyzing the position and dominance of the planets and the overt and hidden sounds within a name, the Naadis can find exactly the right name to achieve optimum benefits.

One of the other delightful things about all this is that the Naadis apply this practice to non-living things as well. It is not just applicable to names. Whatever you need or make use of can be involved – be it a business, a piece of machinery, a car, an asset or anything else that you own. Who needs breakdown cover when your name has been chosen for the great favor it receives from the gods?

Which makes me want to ask where all this leaves me, blessed as I already was with the name Andrew long before I met the Naadis. The subject of names never came up while we were with them, but I have found out since that there may be another way around it that may have been done on my behalf without my realizing it. And for the others who also received their little copper plates from the Naadis once their *puja* had been completed.

It may be that when the priests in Tamil Nadu were doing all that chanting for me twice each day for 192 days, a suitable magical sound might well have been breathed into my little copper plate while it was

being etched, fashioned and prepared (the words and symbols engraved on it being the magical elements applicable to me) and then blessed and chanted over using their special breathing. So when I received it and carried out my own final ceremonies to complete my *puja* it then began to work for me in this way, adding to the power of my penance and my future good fortune. I can't be sure, but I like

Andrew's Naadi Plate to think that's how it works.

CHAPTER SEVEN

Friends' Revelations
Angela:

We made a second mission to India the following year, when we were delighted to offer a select group of close friends the potential to have their palm leaves found in the archives and read, as we had done.

I had written a description of our experiences with the Naadis and sent it to numerous friends, all of whom I felt sure would find it all as intriguing as I had. These were people from all walks of life, most of whom I had originally met through my work as a medium but who had later become good friends. Inspired by our experiences, their responses were quick as most were curious to know about what could be in store for them. Soon we had no less than thirty people hoping for the chance – but there was no way we could consider managing that many people during our trip, particularly when the Naadi holy men were nervous and rather reluctant to undertake what was to them an unusual and strange idea – I had suggested to them doing readings 'by proxy' with me acting in the place of the true seeker or recipient. It seemed they hadn't done it that way before, and to be fair to them it was a tall order given the number of categories and bundles they would need to research, find and then ensure were all in place and ready for each person's quest at their center in New Delhi in time for our visits.

It turned out to be a very trying and exhaustive challenge for every day of the two weeks that we were in Delhi. Even then only five of them were found and only two of these then had their individual leaves suffi-ciently identified to be able to be read in full. For some of the others – whose categories did at least exist (in other words they hadn't been destroyed or lost over time) – I sat for hours in the boiling heat as the Naadi holy man calmly and expertly ran through leaf after leaf with me, bundle after bundle, sometimes getting so very near that surely this or that leaf had to be the one, had to be right... only to then be wrong in one important detail. It seemed that pinpointing the exact person to the leaf was not to be so easily accomplished at that time, and eventually I was told that they would have to send to Tamil Nadu for still more bundles in each of the respective categories if they were to carry on looking.

Politely I tried to put pressure on them to send someone immediately down to Tamil Nadu and get back in a week maybe... But it was more-or-less a case of 'You must be joking!' In India everything is done in a serene, slow and peaceful way, with no stress or rush permitted. I knew it was a three-hour flight south from Delhi, but it seems the Naadis do not fly, so I felt even more duty-bound to make every effort I could to assist my dear friends. All to no avail however, which left me very disappointed.

But the great news was that most of them did at least exist, which meant they could be read at some time in the future... perhaps when they each decided to make the journey for themselves – it would be at the time when it would be their destiny to do so.

Yet it was interesting that the two people who were found were very close to Andrew and I. They were often at our farm in Wiltshire and followed what I would call spiritually enlightened paths (could this have had some bearing on the time being right for them to meet their destiny on the leaves?). But that said, it still took ten hours over two days with Elias at my side to complete their readings and go through the *puja* ceremonies on their behalf, and as I sat there in the sweltering heat hour after hour I thought to myself "Just you wait until I tell you what I've had to go through to get all this done for you both".... It seems my life is one great big *puja*, which tells its own story.

We felt it would fill out the picture of the Naadis a good bit more if we took up the offer of Sheena and Kate to include their own testimonies in this book for you to read. I asked them to write down their reactions to what they were told in their readings. I think you will find them very interesting, even enriching, bringing as they do different and fresh perspectives to the whole Naadi experience. And maybe they will help you decide for yourself about getting your own life reading too.

Sheena shares her Naadi experience

"Soon after Angela and Andrew returned from India in October 2004 I received an email describing their remarkable Naadi experience. I was living in Cairo at the time, where I was teaching Ancient History and Islamic Civilization and researching Ancient Egyptian religion.

I knew nothing of the Naadi astrologers, although I have long been struck by the parallels between Ancient India and Ancient Egypt and their respective mystery schools, so when the chance came to have my thumbprint read in August 2005, I jumped at it. What did I expect? Well, nothing more than I would be delighted if they found my thumbprint ... the rest would be a bonus – and what a bonus it turned out to be!

Naadi to me means 'in pursuit of your soul'. I suppose that has been my sole purpose in this lifetime, an exploration into the mysteries of life and the unseen world of existence. I have a firm belief that we choose our destiny before we are born and that life is the greatest gift to the individual soul to progress on the inner spiritual planes, a cosmic classroom in which we are given a divine opportunity to fast-track our understanding of the Universal Laws of the Spirit if we have the courage to journey within.

'As above, so below' the Ancient Egyptian priests and priestesses taught the young initiates, and as within so without has been my mantra throughout much of my life.

I have had readings in the past and value them enormously as a way of seeing the bigger picture, but I have always trusted my intuition to be the final judge on the decisions I make. So a part of me did not fully appreciate the impact a holy man in India could possibly have on me, let alone believe that he could know any more about me than the broad brushstrokes. Once again I was about to be thrown 'down on the mat'!

To be honest, during the first part of Angela and Andrew's stay in Delhi I didn't really give much thought to what finding my leaf would mean as I was too busy looking after their dogs and catching errant cats to think about it. We would talk on the telephone in the evenings and the news was always the same: "Nothing in Delhi, yet." So when they set off for the second part of their trip up into Kashmir, again with no leaf being found for anyone on their list of friends, I was not really surprised. It was not until the second to last day of their stay in India that I got the telephone call – both Kate's and my leaves had been found, and Angela would be going the next day to hear our fates. Elias, their dear friend, would be on hand to translate.

My reader was nicknamed 'Mr KK'. He began, "*Sheena, your journal chapter is going to be recited*", followed by his name, Mr. K Kolanchi, his address, telephone number and the date, 6th August 2005. After a prayer to Lord Shiva, Mr KK then continued by reciting in a soft sing-song voice the sacred Sanskrit text written on my palm leaf: "*Parvati, Lord Shiva's wife questions Lord Shiva about your predictions for this lifetime.*" So far, so good. Apparently my thumbprint was "*one round shushumareka .... what is written between these lines nobody knows but soon they will come to know.*" It seems it is not a very common thumb impression, which is a source of great amusement to my friends.

Mr KK then questioned Angela as to whether my parents had been aware of the powerful astronomical/cosmological line-up of planets on the day and time I was born. Strange you might think, but not nearly as strange as what it meant to me. In 1994, long after my father's death, I was deeply touched to read the record of my birth in his diary: "*A baby girl, Sheena, arrived at 12.05 midday. The sun shone brilliantly, the sky was a wonderful blue .... A good omen.*"

I had told Angela of this, so when Mr KK asked her she was able to tell him that my father had known. But how on earth could the Naadis have possibly invented or otherwise known about that one?

It was only the first of many staggering accuracies that Mr KK was able to pinpoint from my leaf. I had two marks or '*tulas*' on my thumbprint, one was good, one was bad. Whatever problems I had faced in my life over the past years or was facing now were because of the bad mark on my thumb impression. Had my sins from a past life contributed to this?

"*You were born in Tamil year 'Servadari', in Tamil month 'Aipasse' under Tamil star 'Chittrai'. You have Libra in your birth sign ...*"

This was interesting, since my birth date is 31st October, which in western astrology makes my birth sign Scorpio. I had heard that oriental astrology differed slightly and here it was confirmed. "*At the time of your birth there were 12 oxes in 12 houses, 9 planets in these positions – Aries in Rahu, Leo in Saturn, Virgo, Venus and Mercury in Libra, Sun and Moon in Libra, Scorpio in Mars, Jupiter in Sagittarius. On the date of your birth the planetary positions were such that you were born into a very good family with good luck.*"

"*Father's name Alan, mother's name Doroteeeeee,*" he struggled over the pronunciation. "*One sister married, two brothers, one married, normal education connected to the arts, TV and film, working in the same field, not married but you have a special relationship, you are thinking of leaving your boyfriend. You do not own your own house. You are trying to leave the country where you are living, but it's not happening. You are putting a lot of work and energy into projects but they're not material- izing.*"

Extraordinary – on every detail Mr KK was correct. I had been living for the past seven years in Egypt and as well as teaching, I had spent the previous four years working closely with the Egyptian authorities to bring film and TV production to the new film studio in Egypt. But after 9/11 it had proved an uphill task, and as for leaving the country, why would I want to? I had a good job, great apartment and lots of friends. I could honestly say I was more content than at any other time. Or was I? Over the following weeks and months I would be forced to re-examine my life and ask some very profound questions. Was I fulfilling my destiny or was I afraid to take a giant leap of faith into the unknown?

Mr KK continued: "*Your predictions are normal,*" (what he meant by that I still haven't figured out). *"You did not come personally for your fate but your sister Angela came."* How could Lord Shiva have known 5000 years ago that Angela would come in my place at this time? Truly staggering!

"You are carrying some of your last life's sins with you." I believe every human being has a different past life and carries different sins with them. *"When you see your past life, that is how you live your present life. Because of your last life, whatever you have tried to plan in your present life has not happened. You are spending time and money but it is not successful because of this."* Could it really be that all my hard work over the past few years was being sabotaged by my own past actions? Was this proof of karma in action and was it stopping me reach my full potential in this lifetime? What were these sins? I was about to find out

"You are very intelligent but up until today you have not received the success you deserve. People are jealous of you. Sometimes you are too open with your ideas and your heart. Be secretive. Your secrecy is your weapon to success. Do not talk of your success. Keep your plans to yourself until they have happened." Good advice. I had thought it was because I was as a born optimist that I had a tendency to count my chickens before they were hatched and be very open about my plans and ideas. This was something I had to seriously take on board and work at to find the correct balance.

Overall, my health was good but there was a strong warning not to take chemical medicines, something that I well know as I am very allergic to them. Instead, the importance of meditation was stressed. This was a lifetime of creativity and expressing the inner spirit through the arts, and that creativity could be blocked by drugs of any sort.

Mr KK said that to clear my sins I must do *'Ashanti Deeksha Puja'* which comprises offerings to the Gods – the Brahmin priests would undertake this on my behalf. So how had I accumulated all these sins and what were they? I had always considered my life as very happy and fortunate. I have lived what my friends term 'a very colorful life', rich in experiences, travel, relationships and fun. I was born into a comfortably-off family, the youngest of four children (two brothers and one sister), my father was a retired Naval Commander, poet and astronomer, my mother a superb gardener and cook. We lived in a haunted 13th Century Cotswolds manor house in the UK with a wide selection of pets – dogs, cats, ponies, goldfish, hens and a large garden.

My memory is of large family gatherings and scintillating conversations across a broad spectrum of subjects. We were encouraged to form our own opinions, think liberally 'outside of the box'. Curiosity and creativity were the most precious legacies my father felt he could leave us so we were fortunate to have a great education. From my earliest years I could sense the other world and often saw shadowy phantoms on the stairs. The paranormal was distinctly normal to my family. Like the ancient Egyptians (who had no hieroglyph or word for it) I have never believed that 'death' was the end, always that earthly life was just a stage on a much longer eternal path of return to the All.

And so began the predictions for my life: "*You are 57 running 58. You will continue in your same field of work for now but after your 58th birthday your life will change; it will improve. You are very hesitant to make these changes. You are frightened. Someone will have to push you but do not get frightened. The future is great. Not good but great. You will get great help from a lady friend to make this move. You will go northwest from India – UK, Europe, United States or Canada. You have a very, very secret power inside of you, which up until today you have only barely touched. From the age of 58, slowly, slowly it will begin to open up. You must not be frightened or disturbed by this inner power, just stay focused and controlled, meditate, stay calm; it is your natural power. Do not take any medicine. Go through the pain.*"

"*Getting out of financial problems by autumn 2007 but there may be a court case in October/November 2007. Do not get personally involved and it will all be fine.*" At the time of writing this there was no sign of this yet but we shall see over the coming months whether that prediction comes true. Health good. In 2008 I will join up with a girlfriend to help each other and to help others. I will write and produce a successful TV drama for which I will receive an award. My career will grow and my life will get happier and happier. I will begin to write on spiritual things.

The rest of the predictions were also very positive. *"In 2008/9 you will write a book with a friend which will be very successful – think Harry Potter. You can't even think how this will be now – you, writing a book for kids, but you will, you'll see. It will be so successful,"* Mr KK said excitedly. *"From this book everybody will want to get connected. Many people will benefit from this and you will be sending a very positive message to the world. Happiness is the gift of the gods, think happiness, be happiness, happy mind, happy field."*

This was astounding. In the early 1990s a woman had stopped me in Bond Street, London, and said, "I just had to tell you, you will write a very successful book later in your life." I didn't know her but she said she was a psychic and the message for me was so strong she had to stop me. I never saw or spoke to her again and had forgotten all about it until Mr KK's prediction.

From 2010 I will switch to charity/social work, particularly in India, not just giving money but also looking after people. Then in 2011/2012 I will join up with friends to help people including my brothers and sister. It seems there will be some sort of disaster – could this be linked to the 2012 prophecies? We shall just have to wait and see. Throughout, my thinking processes will be changing and maturing, becoming more and more positive as I meditate more.

The last years of my life will be peaceful, happy and I will die a natural death around the age of 70 in 2018. People will be very kind and helpful.

I had heard the good … now I had to listen to the bad. For my inner power to open up, I had to understand the nature of my sins and do *puja* for them, to truly repent of my past misdeeds.

In my last life, Mr KK said that I was a Hindu man living in the forests of Nepal which, apart from my childhood growing up in the country, could explain why I love nature, prefer a diet of fruit and vegetables and have a great interest in Hindu spirituality. I was the head of my family in that lifetime. I was very religious, I prayed a great deal to Lord Shiva in the forests and I had been given some powers but I had abused them. I had become egotistical and arrogant. I thought that no one was as powerful as I was. I did not always respect my parents. I treated my second wife badly. It was a great love affair but I left her and left everything. She married again but was not happy. When she died she prayed to the gods against me and passed her sins to me. I married again but I was not happy with my third wife. I was impatient and aggressive and didn't treat her very well. When she died she too cursed me. One day I found my power was blocked; it had been taken away from me because I had misused it.

I carried these sins into this life. Truly it was a case of learning the lesson of 'Do unto others as you would have done unto you.' I am definitely someone who thrives in a loving and stable relationship and my home life is very important to me. It's a standing joke that my men have often been like Italian cars – fast and unreliable! Yet I chose them this time round to teach me the lesson of patience and commitment, since in my last life I had certainly not learnt it.

Yet all was not lost. Later in this past life I had repented of my sins. I realized how wrong I had been and how I had abused my power. I dedicated the rest of my life to looking after others – feeding the poor, caring for the sick. Apparently I had done many good things and it was for this reason that I had been '*born into a good family and now my life could move forward*'. But first the Brahmin priests would have to intercede with Lord Shiva on my behalf. There was '*plenty, plenty puja*' to do – 240 days and 10,000 rupees worth of offerings for the gods. Poor Brahmin priests, they would need to buy materials for male and female dresses, fruits, sweets, flowers, copper and incense sticks to carry out their prayers and rituals. They would also make some guru offerings. Eleven Brahmin priests would sit every day making 1008 chantings, reciting my name and asking for forgiveness so that my slate could be wiped clean.

And so for five 48-day periods (making up the total 240 days), morning and evening, the Brahmins chanted and prayed for the forgiveness of my sins and the release of my soul. And at the end of each 48-day period they sent me a large envelope containing two small packets of red and white ash from the ceremonial rituals. Unwrapping them with utmost care, I made a sacred ceremony in my Cairo apartment overlooking the desert, lighting a candle and anointing my third eye with the red and white ash. Then I offered prayers and thanksgiving.

I felt an immense sense of gratitude and humility to the amazing Brahmin priests who devote their lives to prayer and service to help humanity. What a choosing of selfless service they make before they incarnate. It was a lesson to me in true spirituality and sacrifice. It put making films in their proper perspective. For my part I was to help three girls from poor families with their wedding trousseau. This was not difficult in a city with as many poor people as Cairo. What for me was so incredible was the way the opportunities presented themselves without me even looking. I also paid for a young Egyptian girl, Youmna, to have English lessons at the British Council in Cairo.

I have played the tape of my reading over and over again, listening to Mr Koki's words and reflecting at a profound level on my hopes, my fears, my aspirations, my core belief and commitment, my true will and intention. With knowledge of my past life now before me, I was forced to look at my present life under the microscope. Was I still repeating old negative patterns? I had to admit that in this life I had often been arrogant, opinionated and selfish, and that although I was on the surface supremely confident, deep down I was shy and did not truly believe in myself.

My relationships, although powerful and at the time deeply loving, had not lasted. I had left my partners and they had left me. Astonishingly, the second and most powerful love of my life I had left with nothing but a suitcase – just as I had left my second wife in my last life. I had sometimes taken my parents for granted, not always respecting them. I had not really appreciated how lucky I was to have had such a fortunate start in life – a happy secure home, a great education and a positive outlook on life. The similarities between my lives were too great not to be considered. No one was stopping me fulfilling my potential. I was responsible for each and everything that had happened. To be ignorant is one thing, but to be aware and still continue to make the same mistakes is foolish in the extreme. It was time to take a good long look at my life, however painful that might be and to make some changes.

Finally in May 2006, my *puja* was completed and my copper plate was ready for collection. Angela and Andrew brought it back from India for me. It is a small rectangle, just over an inch wide by nearly two inches long. Engraved on it are a number of symbols, a secret alphabet perhaps, a mystery to be discovered. Framed, it stands in the sacred space I have made for it on my desk, a constant inspiration as I sit and write and a reminder of how much life has given to me. There were times at the beginning of the *puja* that I felt unusually low and this spurred me on to increase my meditation practice.

During the whole process I was moved to think deeply about what 'repentance for past sins' means. How could I judge someone else's actions when I had been so ignorant of the underlying motives behind my own? How can we ever know another's journey? My belief in the eternal nature of the Spirit has become a firm conviction. It is my opinion that our souls do live on after death, that what we do in our lives plays an important part not only after our death but also in our future lives; that there is an ongoing eternal process of spiritual enlightenment, just as the Ancient Egyptians knew. My Naadi experience has only strongly reinforced this for me.

Over the past year, as the Naadis predicted, many changes have taken place. From the moment I touched down in Cairo on a steaming August night in 2005, the signs were there that I was coming to the end of my stay in Egypt – being locked out of my apartment, problems with electrical appliances and plumbing, problems with my work visa and my contract at school. My resolve was that if this was to be my last year in that wonderful country, then I would make sure that every minute was precious, that it would be my best year ever – and it was!

I was immensely blessed to have a very positive reading. It confirmed all that I had been thinking and gave me the inner strength and courage to jump off the cliff and follow my heart, to do what I really love. I have left teaching and am writing full time and making films that reflect the Spirit as was written on my leaf. I have just completed a screenplay and am now co-writing a book and drama documentary. I have moved back to Europe from the Middle East to live, and my spiritual journey has broadened out into new avenues and perceptions, just as the Naadis forecasted. As for the rest, we'll just have to wait and see how it all unfolds …

I am currently planning a trip to India to visit a temple in Tamil Nadu, Tirupati in Chitoor district, the temple of Vishnu as Lord Venkatesha. According to the Puranas, Vishnu resided here for the good of humanity. It is one of the most important sites of pilgrimage in southern India and one of the most visited. It stands on the sacred hill of Tirumalai which is considered so holy that visitors may not wear shoes or pick the flowers. The temple itself was only built in the eighth century AD but it has been a place of worship for thousands of years. Mr KK says it is important to me on my life's journey. So watch this space…

As my life unfolds before me, what amazes me is how 5,000 years ago a great sage knew I would come in 2005 to hear my destiny! Truly, the Naadi palm-leaves are one of the Seven Wonders of the Ancient and Modern World, along with the Pyramids. Thank you Angela and Andrew, without you guys I'd never have been any the wiser!

Sheena Mac Brayne

Kate Tells Her Story

Forever it seems I've been fascinated by all things spiritual and have never been one to resist fortunetellers, tarot readers or palmists. I always read the first few pages of a book, then the last few, and only then the middle. I've always wanted to know more, to be attached to the outcome. I have always felt there must be more to life than this, that maybe I was missing my life's purpose.

I've known Angela for many years, she was my first employer when I had completed my training as a riding instructress, and we remained friends even when our paths went in different directions. Some years later I met Andrew, when my family and I moved to Gloucestershire. My husband worked for them for a while on their farm and now I help Angela with her horses. My spiritual interest continued and I have had great help and support from Angela on my spiritual path.

When I first heard about the Holy Men in India I was so excited. Angela and Andrew had visited India and had gone to Delhi to have their palm leaves read. On their return they told us about the Holy men and the palm leaves, I found it unbelievable. It simply blew me away. I was completely fascinated. Could I have mine read? At that moment in time, going to India was as close for me as flying to the moon. Would it be possible for them to do it on my behalf? They said they would ring a friend of theirs, Elias, in India and ask if it was possible, whether that ever been done before. He told them they had never been asked to do such a thing before but they would try, but no promises.

The next time Angela and Andrew visited India they went armed with various people's details and prints of their thumbs. This alone was not easy, the print had to be clear enough for the Holy men to read, as there were no second chances if it was wrong and you were several thousand miles away. Angela knew enough information and knowledge of each person to have his or her palm leaves pinned down. This had never been done before so nobody knew whether it would be possible or not, apart from the fact that not everybody's leaf is ever found, perhaps you are not ready or it is not the right time in your life for it to be found. Until you do this, accepting the possibility that it could be you or it may not be you, you don't really realize the enormity of what you have asked to happen.

There are huge mixed emotions – excitement, fear, trepidation, do you really want to know all that? What do you need to know? Was it even OK to know? You think you are ready to hear all, to embrace all that you need, but they may not find your leaf – oh well, let's go with the flow and whatever is, is.

I think, on reflection, I had no idea of the impact this leaf if found was to have on my life. I personally think that anyone wishing to do this should think long and hard and understand the reason they have the need to find out and whether they are prepared to hear some things they may not want to hear? The good is always balanced by the not-so-good – are you truly ready for the lessons and journeys this may take you on?

When the call came from Delhi: "They've found your leaf!" it felt brilliant, fantastic – how exciting and how scary. "Am I ready for this?" I wondered. "Too late," I cried. Be careful what you wish for, for you may get it.

Then there was the wait! Bless them, Angela and Andrew needed to finish their holiday. Angela was exhausted from sitting with the holy men in India's boiling hot heat for hour after hour – two long days in all, with Angela verifying details through Elias, who very kindly acted as the interpreter for all those hours. If I forgot to say so at the time, 'Thanks guys, I will always be grateful and honored to be one of those very few who were found in a rather unusual way, and one that was beyond the ordinary call of duty in the friendship stakes, to say the least."

When you first receive your tape and sit down to listen to it, if you had not been party to the leaf being found then you have no idea what to expect. And you have no idea of the ceremonies that are performed in your absence for you to be able to even receive it.

When the tape begins you hear all sorts of people talking beyond your comprehension, in their own language, with an interpreter. They are identifying who you are, what the planets were doing when you were born and so on. Now, for the cynics among us, although Angela knew a fair amount about me from our being close friends, there was some information that she didn't know and had no need to know because it either wasn't important or there had been no need for her to know. But it came up and required clarifying, proving that indeed this was my leaf.

How weird it is to hear about your mother, father, their marriage status and retirement. My family is fairly colorful (let's say, 'interesting'). They then moved on to my life, my marriages, my husband's marriages, our life so far, our life together – umm, *"misunderstanding with husband"* rang out at fairly regular intervals, bless them.

I live this life with a fair amount of things not going according to the perfect plan. Well, we will find out why, but from June 2005 they said I will have seven and a half years of *"difficulties"*. No, surely not, that's only just started. This is from past life problems as well as things in this life, yet you really don't expect to hear that your past actions are to be paid for throughout this life, or that if you manage to get away with it this time round then you will still have to pay that debt back next time.

My husband Bernie was listening to the tape and needed convincing that this was all genuine. Strangely, it was at the point when some bad things came up on the tape that was exactly when he really started believing. He is used to me coming back from a reading with everything being jolly and that we will live happily ever after with no slips. So strange as it was, from that point on he sat up and listened hard.

Now, without going into detail, while some of these moments will not be so pleasant, it seems you can do something to lessen their impact by the very fact that you have absorbed what you have done wrong. This all helps.

As with anything that is personal to just you, what shocks is sometimes the minor things. For instance, since I was a child I have always had a minor heart problem and was treated for it. Over the years I have managed to live with it, but more often than not I get heart pains of varying degrees depending what was going on in my life, stress, or even extreme weather. So I have always assumed rightly or wrongly that my heart would be the thing that takes me out. But in the Naadi reading there was no mention of my heart being a problem, and since that day I have had no heart pains whatsoever. Call it coincidence? I don't think so. I believe it was held in my subconscious. Why I held onto the pain I really don't know, but I'm glad it has gone.

Many things were said in that reading of the past, present and future. The past was certainly true, the present I'm beginning to recognize, the future I seriously hope to be true.

Some things have happened already, like "*a fraudulent act*" against me – this was when my handbag was stolen and a card used to get money; "*Husband will have eye problem...*" He is generally pretty unlucky with his eyes but this was really unlucky – he went shooting and the shot hit a tree and came back straight into his eye, causing lots of damage which is still being treated. "*Father heart problem*"... He has since been in hospital due to his heart.

So I can only tick the boxes as we go along.

On the other side of the tape is my last life, the one that affects this lifetime. I had not given a great deal of thought to this part of it to be honest. Things that happen in this lifetime may well make you comment that, "You must have been wicked in a past life". But, for example, I can't bear anything round my neck; the Naadis said I'd "*probably been hung in a previous life*", so maybe never a truer word spoken.

Then the tape began again with *pujas*, the prayers that are said to take away or lessen the mistakes or sins you have made. I am mortified to say I have many sins requiring days and days of *puja*, to be exact 240 days in all, during which some darling holy men will say prayers on my behalf in a specific temple in southern India. This is all to deal with my past life's upsets brought forward to this life, and learning the lessons about them.

"*You were a medicine woman,*" the tape said, as I preened myself like a peacock. Indeed I was a medicine woman in a previous life, I just knew it, as my head swelled even more. But the next words brought me back down to earth with a bump. "*Very greedy*," it said. What me? Yes, "*greedy and unkind*". Surely not. Well, to cut a long story short it seems I held a very good position, but I was mean to my husband and my children and took poor people's money from them as their medicine woman but then did not deliver the goods, keeping the money and making them suffer even more. Funnily enough, in this life someone did that to me and I was outraged, furious and offended, it caused me to get on my soap-box for weeks and I couldn't understand why no one else seemed that bothered. I guess it touched something in my soul. Anyway, later in that past life I apparently realized the error of my ways and tried to rectify things, so by doing that it helped a bit. But I need to sort it fully this time round.

The *pujas* were quite serious but let me tell you if you have taken things this far and heard what I'd heard, you are not going to take a single chance not to make amends. The prayers were to be said constantly in the temple for 240 days with the offerings to the Gods, and for my part I did my prayers daily to Lord Shiva, praying with a lighted candle. Every Saturday I was to fast to the extent that I was not allowed anything that is grown in the ground.

I would be lying to say I stuck to this; towards the end I forgot sometimes. I also had to visit a temple or church on Fridays, and although I did this, it wasn't always on a Friday but it was at least weekly and I always said sorry in my prayers if it was the wrong day and hoped they understood.

I still need to visit a specific temple in southern India during this lifetime, which I will do without question. I entered this life knowing that I was to clear my past and start the next with a clean slate. So I must, and apart from needing to, I wish to.

To sum this journey up, it has had an enormous effect on my life. I understand why I am the way I am over certain issues, and I can only wait and see if what has been predicted comes true. Although I don't sit here waiting for what may be, I naturally still strive to achieve. Maybe I just watch the signposts a little more closely along the way. It has also made me more mindful of others. I have no desire to make friends into enemies, as said in the tape, and if that makes me walk away from an argument with nothing said, then maybe it helps to make this a better place to be.

The *pujas* have had a huge affect on my thinking. Just how many sins do some people have? I didn't consider I was such a bad person, but if all this becomes common knowledge, even if people don't go in search of their own leaf, it might stop them for a moment and make them consider their own actions and that may help make a better place for us all to live. We are all responsible for ourselves, and we all are responsible for our actions. I'm still not perfect by any stretch of the imagination, but I am making an effort. Surely that's a good thing.

Every six weeks I received confirmation of the offerings made to the gods, with a letter of acknowledgement and some powder from the offerings made in payment to acknowledge the sins. It was a milestone each time I received a letter. "More curry powder," my husband said each time one arrived, and it did have the heady smell of incense and the look of, yes, curry powder! When my *puja* was finally complete (which let me tell you takes forever, or so it seems) I received an engraved copper plate, and it was a moment that was very liberating, but after so many days my prayers have since become a ritualistic habit.

A beautiful little copper plate with various markings on it to signify the end of the prayers said on my behalf. I have mine framed and it sits on a table in my bedroom and I look at it daily. It had a huge impact on my life and I believe I am now far more mindful of others. I hope that I have more compassion and understand that my actions do have an impact, not only in my life but on others as well. I am sure everyone has chosen their own paths and are here for their own learning. It feels good to be made aware of my actions. I have every intention of visiting India soon and going to the temple to say my thanks, I feel that it is the least I can do and I won't be doing it because I have to, but because I wish to.

I still visit the church when I go to town. I light candles, say my prayers and thank those heavenly realms for allowing me this wonderful opportunity in this life time to get it right or at least to try to do so. The rest is the future. I will without a doubt be ticking those boxes in the fullness of time, and reflecting occasionally every now and then just to make sure I get it right."

Kate Townsend

I am delighted that Sheena and Kate's Naadi readings meant so much to them, and for the handful of other people we know who have since had their readings done. Yet one of the most telling points all of us have agreed upon is that every time you listen to your taped life story you get something else out of it, something new. You hear it in a different way each time and it seems to expand your learning each time.

I healthily questioned the most significant issues that have come up in all our readings with regard to our past behaviors. I find it interesting that we all have a sense of the memory lurking deep down, so that what we were told regarding previous lives feels absolutely right for each of us.

And the highlight for all of us is to be given what I would like to call 'the opportunity of a lifetime' to truthfully ameliorate all our sins – that's a very big WOW! factor indeed.

We all had the stumbling blocks and problems encountered in this life described in detail on our individual palm leaves. And there is no doubt in any of our minds that they are absolutely correct – it is based on personal background experience and knowledge to date.

Taking it on from there, our own self-evidence kicks in as to what happens next after the *puja* has been done and in the future ahead. In the eight cases that I know well, all of them have so far been 'ticking the boxes' to use Kate's phrase, as the predictions come round and take place. But to confirm any further proof we would need to let time pass and convene again in another few years.

CHAPTER EIGHT

Andrew's View of Temple Architecture

My early Sunday school teachings ground into me that mankind is born with sin whether he (or I) liked it or not, no matter how good I thought I was at the time. The Hindus take a slightly different view, it seems, one that my religious teachers chose to overlook when rolling their eyes and dishing out the brimstone. To Hindus a man's soul is born bearing the good and bad deeds of his past life, so if he'd conducted a good last life then it would naturally reflect in his current life's station and success and vice-versa. I somehow like this idea much better, being now older and wiser, feeling there is a great truth in being kind and considerate to other humans as well as animals and other life forms. Not only does it quickly ground me and give me great satisfaction to do so, but greater hope as well – for us all. Newton proved (scientifically at least) that every action has an equal and opposite reaction, so our sowing badly will surely only reap something equally bad for ourselves if we don't sow well in the first place.

The Hindus therefore see each life as a progression towards enlight-enment, a life-by-life improvement towards ultimate spiritual freedom when the soul finally achieves perfection, united with Spirit, God or whatever you choose to call it. Much of my reading was based on this concept, illuminating the sins I had unknowingly carried with me into this life and the effect they had had on me so far, and what 'Remedies' were then necessary for me to do in order to cleanse and free myself from them, assuring me of a better life next time round, provided I carry on doing good deeds now. It all sounds very prosaic, I know, but for me it's true nevertheless – the feeling of warmth and bonhomie I get from doing even the smallest 'favor' spontaneously to others lasts far longer and feels much greater than the short, bitter, empty pleasure I have had when getting even or worse. But for all that I'm not saying it's easy.

So I'm with the Hindus on this one, even if I didn't appreciate until lately how many gods they have, how their lives were led and how important their temples were and still are to them. And while clearly the Indian temple is not the province of the Naadis alone, there are some fascinating elements behind it that I think you will see are well worth mention.

For the Hindu the temple is the one place on earth where he can cross the divide between the physical and the divine, the place where all physical boundaries can disappear and be transcended. As such it has supreme importance in every aspect of a Hindu's daily life, be it religious, cultural, educational or social. Unlike my own Christian teachings the temple is not just the 'House of God', it is God himself, and has been designed and developed over some 2,000 years to be so, all done in strict accordance with ancient architectural conventions and traditions laid down in the 'Shastras', the age-old texts written by the earliest high priests, the Brahmins.

As a result the temple's evolution has been very conservative and still remains so, for the matter of approaching one's God and sharing in his divine knowledge is indeed a most serious one to the Hindu. To a Hindu, the temple is not just a mere building or even an elaborately constructed, high-soaring cathedral to faith like Chartres or St Peter's – it is all of these and so much more.

In effect the temple has been designed and constructed as a microcosm of the Universe, so that every aspect of its presence on Earth is deemed crucial – the site itself, how it is laid out floor by floor, the size, location, shape and progression of each of its spaces, rooms and corridors, on plan and three-dimensionally, the intricacy of decoration (or the lack of it) and the colors used in finishing. Every aspect of the design has deep-seated meaning and relevance, following religious models and ideologies that have remained unchanged for centuries. To the Hindu, the temple, the physical representation of God on Earth, must not only reflect the Universe all around it, but at the same time adhere to the religious codes and tenets that have fashioned it.

The site itself has to be pleasing to be chosen in the first place. The *'Puranas'* – believed to be the richest collection of mythology known to humankind, completed around 500 AD having been handed down orally by the Brahmins for some 2,000 years beforehand – declare that "the gods always play where groves are near rivers, mountains and springs". Consequently, temples in India tend to be near lakes and rivers for shade and water, all of which are seen to have cleansing and purifying properties. The river Ganges is believed to have come from the heavens, even from the Milky Way, for which reason its water is seen as sacred and so stored in temple reservoirs.

Mountains too have great significance. It was on Mount Kailasa in the Himalayas that Lord Shiva is said to have had his celestial abode, so the mountain has to be represented symbolically in temple construction and finishing – the soaring towers found in so many temples, many of which were painted white originally to appear even more akin to snow-covered peaks, are direct throwbacks to this idea, their dramatic upward movement directly above the pilgrim's head reinforcing the dizzy heights of true enlightenment that he must attain.

Caves are another fundamental, being thought to have the greatest sanctity. The earliest surviving Hindu, Buddhist and Jain shrines are found in caves specifically cut out for that purpose. This provided a heritage that is still followed through today; the *'garbagriha'* in later Hindu temples is the most sacred part of the whole site and is designed as a small, dark cave with unadorned rough-hewn walls and ceiling. To reach it a pilgrim must first pass through the impressive outer gates and open, inner courtyard areas until, via a succession of progressively smaller, darker, less-decorated and simpler spaces, he finally reaches the sanctuary itself (the *'garbagriha'*) by which time the structural fabric and form – and he himself in theory – have been stripped bare of any remaining pretence and grandeur and are naked of all coverings and alone with God.

But it didn't stop there. The ground plan was crucial in other ways too, not only in the way the pilgrim approached the cave. Again the *Shastras* had dictated the layout, likening it once more to a microcosm of the Cosmos. Here the basic shapes that could be used could only be rectangular, elliptical, circular, octagonal or square, depending upon the deity that the temple housed. So a reclining god such as Ranganatha, for example, could only be accommodated by a rectangular shape.

Even so, circular and octagonal shapes are apparently very rare. It seems that to the Brahmin priest, the square was the most sacrosanct of shapes, if not almost mystical. As a result the grid their architects tended to use was based on a *mandala* of 64 or 81 squares, each one having its own significance and corresponding deity, with all of them in turn of greater importance and divinity the closer to the center they were placed, with the center square housing the ultimate – the deity of the temple itself.

The *Shastras* also dictated that the principal shrine would always be built with its entrance facing east, towards the sunrise, with access to it made along the east-west axis through a series of ever more important spaces deliberately enhanced and heightened by the complexity of the architecture and the structural form around them. So, by design and the careful use of decoration, shape, light and volume, the Hindu pilgrim would move in the time-honored way from the open, physical world into the serene, divine eternal, passing first through the entrance, usually covered by a porch or decorated gate and very often with a high tower or *'mandapa'* rising above it, then on through carefully graded internal spaces finally to reach the dark inner sanctum, the *'garbagriha'* or 'womb chamber', with its own tower rising above it up to the heavens.

* * *

The *Shastras* generally classified temples into three different styles and orders – the *'Nagara'* type found in northern India, the *'Dravida'* type found in southern India, and the *'Deccan'* or *'Vesara'* type found in the area between the two, and as a result naturally much more of a hybrid form. There are others too, as with the types found in Kerala, Bengal and the Himalayas, but by far the most of the temples that have been built are in the above three styles.

The *Nagara* style evolved in the 5th Century AD and can best be characterized by a beehive shaped tower comprising several layers of what look like dormer windows overtopped by a large round cushion-like element called an '*amalka*', all based on a square ground plan. The *Dravida* style, deriving from the 7th Century AD, has a pyramid shaped tower, comprised of successively smaller stories of small pavilions with a dome over the top called a '*shikhara.*' The *Deccan* style uses overlaps from each.

The raw materials prevalent in each region would have significant effect on how the temple was built and formed, as well as the style and quality of its decoration and carving, affecting its whole appearance. Softer stone areas would permit the sculpture to be far more detailed and intricate, matching ornate work found in ivory or sandalwood, while harder stone areas would only allow the lightest and most shallow relief carvings by comparison. In areas where there was no stone, such as Bengal, temples were built of brick and would be different again, responding directly to the natural abilities that this material held.

But history has its claim over both art and religion. Some of the elements and decorative aspects found in the very earliest temples still had to be slavishly repeated even though the reason and meaning for them might have been lost. The details that would have been found in the early timber and thatch temples are still there in the stone-built ones, but in symbolic form – as with the 'horseshoe' window, whose origins are 3rd Century BC but which later became the dormer window or '*gavaksha*' and then, later still, a purely decorative pattern on the towers of medieval temples. Conservatism was all-important in following the rigid precepts of the ancient *Shastras*, so tradition alone would dictate the continuing use of post, beam and corbelled vaulting methods of construction rather than anything more modern.

Yet the most distinctive difference between the northern *Nagara* and southern *Dravida* types of temple are the gateways. In northern India these are unassuming and modest with the bias instead on the domed centerpiece of the temple itself, whilst in the south, where the whole temple complex is enclosed by surrounding walls, it is the gateways or *'gopurams'* with their barrel-shaped roofs, that hold center stage, being by far the most prominent element as they rise ever taller and taller – as much as 190 feet in the case of the Tanjore temple – to become the most striking feature of the whole site, clearly seen from miles away, dominating the whole locality in general and the temple's inner sanctum in particular. From the 16th Century onwards these became ever more embellished with sculpted, lifelike figures all decorated in the very brightest of colors, as maintained to this day.

From the 8th Century AD religious rituals became progressively more elaborate. This was reflected in temple architecture, particularly in the south where more and more towers or *'mandapas'* were required for the various ancillary purposes such as assembly, eating, dancing, and even a stable for Lord Shiva's sacred horse. This resulted in still more corridors and shrines and culminated in the emergence of the 'thousand-pillared halls', the largest of which is at the Dravidian temple of Meenakshi at Madurai built in the 17th Century. This has the tallest *'gopuram'* in the world and comprises over 2,000 pillars, each richly covered with carvings full of rampant figures, rearing lions, fearsome elephants and all manner of strange beasts and things.

Not quite everything was determined by the *Shastras*. Subject to the material from which the temple was built there were still freedoms permitted in the extent and means of decoration and embellishment that could then be put upon it. For which reason very many temples – indeed all those that generally spring to mind when one thinks of them – have a riot of sculpture and intricately carved figures prancing and climbing all over them, some depicted in conservative ways, some in glorious battle scenes, some with hordes of animals, and some outrageously erotic and degenerate to the Victorian English eyes that rediscovered them in the late 19th Century, when the overtly sexual nature of the works found on some prominent southern Indian temples were deliberately overlooked and ignored by the British explorers wishing to spare female blushes.

* * *

Patronage has always been an important factor in temple construction. It never was the architect, sculptor or painter who was immortalized for their work and skill in building them, for nearly all Hindu art is anonymous. Instead it was and still is the patrons who are honored, whether they be royal (as once they were) or as they are now, private individuals who are celebrated. This not only had great affect upon the style in which the temples were built, reflecting the wishes of the particular dynasty that built them – whether Chola, Hoysala, Gupta, Pallava or Chandella – but also in other ways. So a donor interested in achieving as much spiritual forgiveness and enlightenment as he or she could obtain through the *puja* it would attract might well give their temple gold, silver or money – even livestock or the income from villages that they owned.

Naturally such great patronage in turn led to the most valued temples becoming like small cities in themselves, entire communities that hired priests as well as suppliers of the produce necessary for offerings for their valuable work and sacred rituals – garlands, milk, ghee, fruit, rice, oil, incense, sandalwood. In 1011 AD the temple of Rajarajaeswara in Tanjore listed "dancing-girls, dancing-masters, singers, drummers, conch-blowers, accountants, parasol-bearers, lamp-lighters, water-sprinklers, potters, carpenters, astrologers, tailors and jewel-stitchers" on their books – more than 600 persons in all, which sounds to me to be very much as a hypermarket would be today, giving life and livelihoods to all who lived, served or relocated themselves to suit nearby. Some even gave grants of land to those that served them, for them then to cultivate and use.

Small wonder then that the temples became very wealthy. One of the wealthiest – and most charitable – around today is apparently at Tirumala, where 30,000 pilgrims are said to visit daily, the staff number some 6,000 and the revenue is around $165 million per annum and no doubt rising.

Busy places indeed. All of this still goes on, day in, day out. I remember an occasion when Angela and I were out on the road coming back from the Taj Mahal with our Hindu guide and driver. Without any warning we suddenly pulled off the road and braked to a halt outside a large temple that we had passed on the way out, our guide explaining to us that he and the driver had to make donations before the day was out. We sat and watched while we waited for them to return. All the time there was a constant stream of traffic stopping and pulling up, with each driver or passenger getting out to put money in the box provided, then returning to their vehicles and starting off again with much hooting, pulling out and getting in everyone's way. No matter, it was all taken very seriously indeed, and life continues like that all the time. That is how the priests and staff survive – without such donations they could not be housed, fed, clothed or employed.

Which brings me back to the present day. Whilst we met our Naadis in New Delhi it is actually in the state of Tamil Nadu in southern India that they have their spiritual home. It is a province that boasts literally thousands of temples, for the Tamils were the greatest of the temple builders, raising and constructing them from pre-Christian times until almost the present day. Some of their structures have survived intact for over 1,700 years, testaments not only to the faith behind them but to the craftsmanship, dedication and skill of all those that fashioned, built and worked upon them, enabling even those of humble means to approach his god or gods in the way he must.

* * *

Brahmin Priests

What of the priests that serve the temples, the sages that undertook all that chanting on my behalf in Tamil Nadu whilst I did my *puja*? They are Brahmins, the name meaning literally 'knowers of God', members of a stratum of Hindu society found particularly in India and Nepal. To all Brahmins, God is one, but He can have many names and forms to worship in line with the different languages, cultures and varying perceptions of how He is seen. To Brahmins, religion is not man-made but revealed through truths deemed to have eternal relevance and ultimate validity.

Originally a 'Brahmin' would mean an initiate of or learned individual expert in the *Vedas,* the holy scriptures that are the source of all Brahmin traditions and practices. For this reason, if not ascetics, they generally became teachers and advisors to the ruling class, the Kshatriyas, and provided they were proficient in religious knowledge there was no bar as to which class or caste they came from – high skill in priestly duties was all that was required to rise to the top, with spiritual knowledge prized far higher than lineage, allowing a Brahmin priest to rise above his lowly birth or station.

One needs to remember that Hindu society is divided into a caste system with four '*varnas*' or levels. The first and most important is the '*Brahmins*', the scholars responsible for guarding all spiritual matters and technical knowledge; the second is the '*Kshatriyas,*' the warriors and ruling class; the third is the '*Vaishyas*' or agricultural and merchant class, and finally there is the '*Shudras*', the working or manual labor class.

Traditionally, the Brahmins have always been priests but Indian society has more recently found them in other callings and professions – clerks, administrators, academics, journalists, industrialists, scientists, militarists, Nobel Prize winners and even Prime Ministers, Nehru and Indira Gandhi to name two. While comprising only a small percentage of the general population (between 2-5% in the whole of India) they continue to contribute greatly to Hindu culture.

In essence the Brahmin has six principal duties – learning, teaching, making sacrifices to the gods by placing offerings of fruits, coconuts, grain, clothing etc into the divine fire, (just as my Naadi reader did for me in my 'Remedies' ceremony, which I then had to repeat in order to officially start my *puja)*, studying and chanting the Vedas, accepting gifts and donations and finally giving gifts or making donations to others, (as with the money and other offerings I had to make to the gods in my ceremony). As in Buddhism, the belief is that the more one gives without seeking or expecting any return, the wealthier one will become.

To carry out all of these duties the Brahmin priest needs great discipline, for it is a harsh and unrelenting routine that occupies every part of his day and follows a strict order. The vocation he has chosen is one of hardship and austerity. His day begins early – he rises two hours before dawn, cleans his teeth, bathes in cold water and then, once pure in body, he must commence his first sacrifice of the day at dawn. Thereafter he studies and chants the Vedas to attain and maintain the purity of his mind, learning the ancient knowledge which he will then teach to his disciples. Thereafter he must gather flowers and bathe again before making whatever *puja* he has to perform – his moment for prayer, worship and showing respect and contrition to the gods – all of which has to done before eating.

He must beg for his food as well as for the offerings and materials he will need for the two sacrifices he has to make daily at dawn and dusk. But it is his right to do so as he is not paid any salary and likely has no other means of support. That said he is only permitted to beg for the minimum amount required to keep him and his sacrifices going, and any surplus will be taken up either by the priests who officiate with him at the sacrifices or by his next duty, which is to give charity himself and make donations to others. Life for a Brahmin it seems is forever close to the edge.

Once these tasks have been completed, the Brahmin must bathe yet again and pray to his fathers and follow this with still more *puja*, dedicating all objects he can see with his five physical senses to the gods.

By now it is around midday. Only now will he have completed the daily rites to the gods, the Vedas and the fathers that he is required to do – and he has yet to eat. But before doing so, first he must honor and feed any guests as well as the 'creatures of the earth' and the poor. This he does by offering rice to the sacrificial fire, then leaves it about the place for the beggars, dogs, birds and outcasts to find and eat – all done with chanting – after which he must entertain the guests. It is then, and only then, that he himself can take food, apart maybe from a little milk or buttermilk if he can find the time beforehand. Brahmins are not permitted to snack.

After his lunchtime meal he must then read the *Puranas* and continue teaching for whatever remains of the afternoon, this time to members of the other castes. Once completed, he must take his evening bath to purify himself again before making his final sacrifice of the day. After this he can have his evening meal, comprising light food only such as fruits and milk, and retire to bed.

Not an easy life, I'm sure you'll agree, for clearly there's no moment or period allowed when the Brahmin priest can relax or rest in any day. No weekends off or holidays for them. But on finding this out, it did make sense to me when I thought back to the Naadi holy men I'd met in Delhi, and how polite, deferential, serene and somehow detached they always appeared to be.

They were charming and amusing too, and even a bit excitable like children when the leaves were found – but for all that they were never less than very disciplined in mind and the following of ritual, and they went through the whole Naadi process with us calmly, quietly and very professionally, exuding an air of great spirituality throughout. Even when they laughed or giggled, as occasionally they did when they saw our faces look back in wonder and awe at what we were hearing and finding out from our leaves.

My respect for the Naadi priests has only increased with knowledge and time, for it tells me that the true Naadi readers are most certainly not opportunists who have managed to complete a hasty two-week course somewhere in 'How to Read Palm-Leaves' and then stuck up a sign, but instead are deeply dedicated and professional individuals with great esoteric knowledge and who are there purely for the service of others.

So while it may appear to the seeker sitting on the other side of the table that reading the leaves is purely a mechanical, interpretative process of going through the right motions, I'm convinced that this is not the case at all, for a lifetime's ongoing training in the Brahmin traditions has undoubtedly proceeded your appointment with each bona fide Naadi reader you meet, let alone all the study he has been required to do in order to properly and faithfully read what destiny and the heavens foretell.

So beware any and all charlatans who offer quick fixes...

CHAPTER NINE

What The Global Records Reveal for the World
Angela:

My life's journey is a spiritual one but for Andrew his answer to that would possibly be "still under consideration". I have always seen the world as one big picture within my sights, so it was without question that I would be asking the Naadis for a global reading covering the salient points over the next 10 to 11 years from 2007 to 2018.

I understood that it was not going to be easy to get this information, not because it didn't exist but because the actual palm leaves that are written up on the world are not shared amongst the Naadi readers. To do so they are not looking at individual thumbprints and searching for their categories, rather the astronomical calculations that were given thousands of years ago and written up on regions of the globe based on specific issues that would effect the population.

As Andrew has explained, there are numerous ancient palm leaves on Vedic writings regarding health, astrology, medicine and mathematics, all based on astrological and astronomical calculations, and many of these are presently being deciphered, carefully preserved and catalogued by a handful of trained students at Madras University. They believe it is going to take them many years to complete the task. But the writings I am interested in are still held with the Tamil families and are very closely guarded.

I was inspired by a man called Dr B V Raman who in 1950 wrote in the Astrological Magazine of India:

"Kaka Bujander Naadi deals with such topics as astronomy, international affairs, the spiritual elevation of mankind and so many other things in which humanity is interested. One cannot but admire a system of literature, written thousands of years ago and containing

references to current and future international problems. "

Dr Raman also cited a brief and delightful sample of a Naadi reading that had been done in the early 1900s:

"The native will be born in a holy city on the coast of the ocean. At the age of 20 he will go to a foreign country. His mother will die at the age of 22 in his absence. He will marry at 13. At 32 he will be a lawyer. He will always speak the truth and will be pure in heart. There will be no distinction between his thoughts, words and deeds. Before the age of 65 he will meet the King of the white race. He will resort to fasting for the good of the world. He will live beyond the age of 70. "

This is the palm-leaf reading belonging to Mahatma Gandhi!

During my research I had come across a couple of old books in India printed over 50 years ago speaking on the subject, so I was determined to find the Naadis who knew so much more about it all and could read the predictions. I was well aware that it wouldn't be easy but the way the palm leaves are written for individuals made it reasonable and logical that the same technique would have been used based on a similar system to categorise the regions of the world. In this way the world would be divided up into sections such as: *'2 countries East of India'*, *'12 countries West of India'*, or an *'area to the North'*. After all, they were utilizing the planetary aspects for specific times in the *Kandams* for war, the economy, health and representing earth, fire, and water.

Through the readings we have already covered I came to understand that there is a sense of great alteration and change due in the world during our time. That feeling seems to be affecting a great number of people, and perhaps more than ever before there is a 'wanting to know' and searching for answers to their origins and a wish to find their spiritual roots. Some are accepting the idea of living many lives and deaths to reach their nirvana of existence before finally 'going back home'.

Predictions for The World

From what I understood, the calculations covering the Earth are based on the placement of planets at a specific time ahead. They tell a story of a great and grave upheaval, first economically and then politically, that would resonate across the globe, and there will be times of danger from two warring factions fighting for supremacy in three regions of the world.

In addition, major climatic changes are foreseen due to the Sun – the extreme times (as calculated) taking place first in 2009 and secondly between the end of 2011 to 2013. The continent of Asia will suffer in particular.

The Middle-East and Northern regions will experience two geological shifts when the Earth itself will move. Water will be involved on both occasions.

Before and after these times, however, the people will be guided, aided and directed to understand what is happening and learn from the experience.

* * *

I gave a lot of thought to these pointers and on reflection I believe the world's history offers a much worse picture than the future holds. For a start, there has never been 'peace on earth' – there has always been at least one or more wars going on somewhere in the world over the centuries. Volcanoes and earthquakes have been regular occurrences, as has flooding in many regions, and whilst I admit they have seemingly been increasing in regularity and size, to me it seems as if everything is expanding in the universe at the same time – including our consciousness.

When it comes to the world economy, over the last hundred years it has been like a roller-coaster ride with numerous financial collapses and recoveries, so there's nothing new there.

But the Sun has perhaps the most significant effect on the whole of the planet. Obviously we rely on it for our survival, so when it starts to cause alterations to the globe we will have to learn to adapt and shift our way of living and thinking. But I am confident that our instinct for survival is truly enormous – it is deeply inbuilt in the human psyche and we will seek new ways of living to follow and suit the changes.

* * *

My next thought was to take all the Naadi readings that I had been privy to – eight in all – and marry them together, the idea being that the years of difficulties should show up in all of them.

The good news is all eight people are alive throughout this 11-year period – and that includes those living in the USA, India, UK and France. So what's the bad news? Well, there are going to be some upheavals, that's for sure. I noted significant predictions in following years illustrating 'happenings' (for want of a better word) where we would individually be giving help and assistance to people in other regions:

2008 - Speaking out on spiritual matters to help inspire people on spiritual matters, including powerful writing and film work.

2009 - The setting up of a charitable foundation to help the peoples in other regions of the world. Giving help to children and the next generations through writing, television and film, so developing and sharing a new way of thinking towards spiritual knowledge and religion. There will be a joining-together of many people, particularly in the younger generation.

2010/11 - Charity and social work involving India and other areas of Asia. Very many people are involved.

2012/13 – Governments appoint individuals to carry out charitable works on their behalf, tying up with groups to help people in many regions of the world. Government funding is included. There will be great communication between peoples across the world.

2013/14 - There will be a need to design and construct unusual new buildings for people in need, all of which will have charitable status. It will be spiritually-based.

2018/20 - Many people are involved and speaking on spiritual matters; much travelling is involved, with more promotion through media, film and the written word. A sense of calm and peace emerges.

So the conclusion of this short period in time seems to be the opening of a doorway into a golden era of openness, understanding and spiritual consciousness.

The eight Naadi readings that I worked with to collate the above information were all for individuals who are closely connected to Andrew and I, so it seemed reasonable there would be a natural progression towards our involvement in the areas of media, writing, television, film and spirituality. But what was quite remarkable was the fact that while none of us are the same age, the timings of what was written on the palm leaf predictions dove-tailed exactly between each of them, year by year, so I truly believe these things are 'written' and will happen as predicted over the next 11 or so years.

Interesting? Only time will tell!

CHAPTER TEN

A Spiritual Awakening
Angela:

After the extraordinary experience Andrew and I had with the Naadis I realized Andrew had made a huge shift in his consciousness. Not only was I watching his view of life change before my eyes but I also kept sensing an incredible overview of the whole design on humanity's destiny.

I just could not stop myself following a spiritual quest. This was to satisfy my deep-seated interest in all things spiritual. Coming from my intuitive way of being throughout this life I needed and called for answers that would satisfy me and that, to a greater extent, could be shared with everyone who wished to take the journey. Those with a strong linear-logical mind may have difficulty accepting the vast potential that is out there by means of this knowledge.

At some time or other we all want to know where we came from, where it all started and how we got here on planet Earth in the first place. To fully comprehend what I am about to share with you, please understand that I believe the physical body is just a vessel that has been carefully engineered to give the soul an opportunity to exist in earthly surrounds every time it wishes to come here and enjoy the physical pleasures. But I for one am convinced that ours is not the first civilisation to exist on this planet, and that the previous one (or ones) made enough mistakes to finish themselves off almost entirely. Hence our great difficulty in proving they ever existed, or the scorn with which concepts and civilizations such as Atlantis are met. I believe we are taking the same road again, and it is only through our searching to know more and change our ways, that we can divert the problem away from our present track and timeline in this unique period in our human history.

I have always been naturally drawn to giving service to people, I guess it goes back to seeing my life as being one big *puja*. I used to joke with clients that I must have done some seriously bad stuff in my previous lives to warrant such a life of service this time round… and I was never actually joking. The Naadis certainly gave me some pointers in this.

Since then I have been drawn towards taking a global overview, rather like being in a plane at 30,000 feet and observing what goes on below. Up there you can feel totally removed from any situation beneath you, which helps your awareness without involvement. So, with little or no attachment to the outcome, I am seeing a very big picture indeed, one that involves all of us living today and, thanks to the Naadis, I am now completing a spiritual pathway which feels like finally putting a ghostly jigsaw together.

As an intuitive, medium and spiritual mentor, I receive messages from those who are not now of this physical dimension but in another, a dimension over and above this one but connected to it from next door. I was born with this natural tuning fork fully activated in my brain and it allows me now to walk a well-trodden path as a receiver and communicator. It takes a tremendous amount of energy to do this work I do and stay healthy, so I quickly learnt how to naturally draw in an abundance of energy wherever I am and expend it whenever necessary for my work.

My practice allows me to transmit strong positive waves of thought out there to tap into the Akashic Records – the records held like an energy disc on all humanity beyond and encircling the planet – rather like clicking on the web. I can then receive visual and thought pulses back in response. I often get far more than I bargained on, for there really is so much out there to digest and absorb.

In just the same way, the mythology that has been handed down over the centuries through ancient Hinduism had made sense to me. I found myself deciphering anew what was fact and what was fiction in a profoundly spiritual way. Scientific evidence giving us the age of the oldest known palm leaves is all very fine and useful but it stops where it does, and that answer was never going to be enough for me. I have no doubt that what is known as the 'occult' today (it actually means 'hidden') will be the science of tomorrow, and I am one of those innovators who has always seen well ahead on our present timeline. So I find it no problem at all to 'look' and 'receive' for other people and I also enjoy getting involved on a very much larger and wider scale.

But now I want to draw you to a distant moment back in time and see the view that I believe comes from the wisdom of those who stood before us, all those centuries ago, who were willing to share the knowledge of life. It is through this view and my perception and understanding of what I am hearing from the God-Source that I have written what you now are reading – so make of it what you will. Deep down you will know if it feels right to you, as it does me.

The 'truth' on humankind was spoken of some 5,000 years ago to the initiates, all of which was then written down on palm leaves some 3,000 years later. Yet it all goes back eons before that, when such things were passed down through speech alone.

The Mysteries

In Hindu mythology there are the ancient stories of the Seven Rishis (seers) and the Hindu Trinity of Lords Brahma, Vishnu and Shiva, the three of whom represented the three fundamental powers made manifest in the world – Creation, Destruction and Maintenance. I see these three having origins that connected them to a doorway or portal in the Himalayan mountains at the very beginnings of time, one that the gods used to travel back and forth to the other dimensions and planets. I believe that portal still exists, together with the technology to work it, but it is way beyond the reach of most ordinary human beings.

It is said that these three gods were to teach and share their knowledge with their followers, leading to the information now found in the writings of India's greatest sages and saints. It was one of these three beings, Lord Shiva, whom we have been writing about, who was the one who gave us the truths of our own lives.

The Story

In southern India around 3000 BC a being arrived from a planet known as the Source of the Universe who took physical form, having chosen to give a lifetime in service to the souls who had and were arriving into the physical bodies of humanity. He was what you would call now one of the greatest Indian sages, one of the very highest order, and perhaps one of the first of three ever recorded in Indian history. He is known throughout ancient Hindu tradition as 'Lord Shiva', the one who took it upon himself whilst in life-form to commune with the God-Source of the Universe from whence he came. He, together with the Lords Brahma and Vishnu, has been enshrouded in ancient Hinduism and respectfully revered by the Hindus ever since. And it is these three that have held the very highest responsibility for the welfare of humanity from that time to this, over all the centuries that separate us.

Whilst living in the physical world these three avatars sought permission to tap into the Akashic Records by 'calling in' for the complete life of the civilisation existing in our own timeline, as they had agreed to do so 'in the most divine way'.

Once this was granted, Lord Shiva vowed to spend his whole life deciphering every piece of information he was given by way of 'divine prophecy', so that every significant detail appertaining to each individual soul could be recorded and written up. This covered their beginnings, their life purpose for each of their lives, their trials and tribulations as well as the duration of their stay for each and every life they were to lead. This was then all documented for each and every soul who was to call upon the knowledge in some later epoch – as we had now done by seeing the Naadis.

It was and still is the very greatest form of divination and oracular guidance, based on the ancient knowledge and spiritual wisdom of Lord Shiva, who understood the planetary system and indeed the planets where the souls of humankind originated. And the knowledge was given in such a way to be illustrated via a mathematical system based on 108 categories covering all humanity, so encompassing every caste or type of human across the world.

These categories were then refined further and deciphered next through specific markings on the thumb of each and every human born into life, taking into account the stage or phase each individual had reached within the cycle of their many lives.

It is from there that each one is then uniquely identified and recognised – their race, creed, personality, families and their names, aims, jobs of work, loves and troubles – leading to the next stage of using fixed astronomical and astrological calculations in order to find and read the horoscope unique to each one.

This was done principally by means of the position of the planets known at the time and whether the Moon was in the Ascendant or Descendant at the precise time of each one's birth. From that point, further computations could then be made to complete a fully detailed life reading, including the character and all the actions each would make.

I understand that all other life forms born into life such as animals, mammals and plants are included in the Akashic Records, but sufficient time was not given for the mammoth task of transcribing all of them as well as all humanity during the lifetime of the three great avatars and their seven principal scribes.

Even so, through Shiva's considerable teachings on astronomy, astrology and mathematics he was able to give his initiates the deepest education of the planets and the effect they have on all life forms, rather like a perfect orchestra playing. This knowledge included health and healing for all and covered the global picture in sections as well as the continents and their future histories in terms of politics, wars and economics.

But Shiva held another awareness, a 'knowing' power, way beyond the ken of the people at that time, and had sense enough to have his works preserved so that they would be carried down through the centuries. It is these that I believe became the 'olas (the palm-leaves) of divine prophecy'.

Language of the gods

This vast, incredible body of work was carried out and eventually translated into the ancient poetic language of the earliest Sanskrit writings, a language known to hold many of the oldest writings known to mankind. The actual word Sanskrit is said to be the 'language of the Gods' and is the most ancient language of India. It actually means 'carefully and accurately polished language' for which reason Sarasvati, the supposed inventor of Sanskrit, is also called the Goddess of Wisdom and Knowledge, and it is claimed that the sages received the Sanskrit characters from Sarasvati herself.

In endeavouring to establish a relationship between the potential timing of these people and their story I must include what I feel is a strong connection with the other main historical writings of India, namely the *Vedas*.

The *Vedas* or '*Puranas*' are the fount of ancient Hindu's divine knowledge. It is the richest collection of Hindu mythology known to humankind. There are many astronomers and mathematicians to this day in India who have undertaken the task of proving to the satisfaction of others that the Vedas are indeed the oldest written works in the world. I am wanting to link the work in the Vedas with the information handed down on the olas which, if correct, would make them possibly the oldest form of divinely-inspired work on humanity's pre-destined lives surviving anywhere.

One of the most well-known scholars of the 1800s, Prof Friedrich Max Muller, the Professor of Comparative Philology at Oxford University, England, helped to establish Sanskrit as a major classical language. Having spent 30 years engaged in translating the full text of the '*Rig-Vedas*' he believed he had the proof of their age and illustrated such in his book titled *Chips from a German Workshop*. In a later, edited version he wrote on the antiquity of the Vedas in *Our Figures*, in which he demonstrated the validity of his calculations in relation to the *Vedas'* age based upon their descriptions of times of great change in the tropics, or Moon phases, or the winter and summer solstices, and the vernal and autumn equinoxes. The ancient *Vedas* recorded all such changes in their writings, changes that could then be checked back and confirmed by other means.

A bit beyond most of us perhaps, but it reminds me of the more recent calculations done on the alignment of the pyramids at Giza, as shown to be in perfect alignment with the relevant planets at a much earlier time than thought possible before, putting it back to a time some 10,500 years ago. To me the question is then whether this was in fact the time of their actual construction or maybe that something even more significant took place on Earth then. It's an intriguing question for me, at least.

Ancient Hindu Trinity

First we have Lord Brahma who in Hindu writings is the 'unseen' God Source, the one who came from there and who is the Creator of the Universe, and Saraswati, who is said to be the inventor of Sanskrit and the Goddess of Wisdom or Knowledge, his wife. This to me means she followed the divine spiritual path communing with the God Source beyond all material and physical desires, dedicating her life in service for the welfare of humanity. And she is depicted holding a bundle of the written 'olas' in one of her hands.

Lord Vishnu, the second of the three, is known as the God of Maintenance and a preserver of the universe. He is strongly believed to have ten avatars (holy descendants on Earth) of which only nine have so far come to Earth, including Lord Krishna and Lord Rama.

Then we come to number three, the great being Lord Shiva, who is known as the God of Destruction, yet the one who achieves inner harmony and maintains perfect calm and serenity. He is depicted in a meditative pose with his home in the background – Mount Kailas in the Himalayas. The Goddess Uma, also known as Frakriti ('all perishable matter') is said to have been wed to Shiva but again I believe that, like Saraswati, she vowed to take the spiritual path beyond all physical desires. To conceal her true nature she was often written with the name Boutos or Bythos, which means 'depth'.

As a trinity these three represent the fundamental laws of Nature and all three are manifest at all times in a fine balancing act of cause and effect, put simply creation, destruction and maintenance.

Then there are the *Septa Rishis*, the seven great Sages, all of whom are held in the very highest regard and are revered to this day. One of them was Kausika, who later became known as Saint Kausika Mashashiva. His students in turn became Adept Masters who passed on the hidden, esoteric knowledge for generation after generation.

And what of the other six? Well they each have a following in their own name with palm leaf readings through the different families. Each of them has a slightly different, varied tradition and training. Naranda Naadi is written up as being one of the physical sons of Brahma. It is said that he was connected through his first incarnation to the seven 'Builders' (called the seven 'Rectors' in the Christian Church) who helped God in the work of creation.

In the early 1900s much research and writing was done by a number of Indian gentlemen who were by then questioning the accuracy and authenticity of the Naadi palm leaf readers based upon the first hand experience that they and their friends had had. Having completed their investigations, they generally agreed that the leaves comprised some of the greatest works known to mankind. I quote: "The irrefutable and unchallengeable feat is that Tamil Naadis use such an enormously large number of terms in Sanskrit as would leave no doubt, whatsoever, that the Tamil Naadis must have been modelled on original works of Sanskrit." One form of Tamil script is known as the *Naadi Grantha Lipi*, which is still written in Sanskrit.

There are other fascinating connections too regarding the use of leaves to make and preserve written works of the earliest origin. The first is the

Book of Enoch. It is said that this again was of Indian origin and dated back to an epoch long before Moses. But more importantly it was written down on detached palm leaves believed to be of fine gold and precious metals. These metallic leaves were said to be original and so escaped destruction during 'the deluge' – possibly The Flood.

A second leaf connection is with the *Adi*, the generic name of all the first speaking races in each of the seven zones of the world or continents. Such 'first men' in every nation were credited with being the first to be taught the divine mysteries of creation. Then according to the Sufis, the Sabeans hold that when the third 'first man' left the country adjacent to India (ie. the Himalayas) to journey to Babel, a tree was given to him, then another, and then a third tree whose *leaves recorded the history of all the races*. So it seems that leaves were a natural medium for the very earliest writings. Yet here we are today with our modern technology still using reams of paper, only one step away in one sense from those very ancient originals.

By now I was also interested in finding anything I could that would support India having been the fount of much more than the earliest use of leaves for writing upon.

Forefathers of the Hindus

There's a school of belief that Hercules was of Indian origin, and that he was in fact Krishna's brother Baladeva. This is reflected in the Vedas, most of which attained final written form between 300-500 AD but which had previously been passed down orally by the elders since the time of Krishna. It seems that the ancient classical writers understood Hercules' Indian origins so well that they unanimously attributed him to an Asian background, and in occult doctrine it is told that Hercules was actually the last incarnation of one of the seven "Lords of the Flame". It all starts to ring a bell for me, but then I am one who can accept re-incarnation, many lives and many faces.

I also found myself asking whether some of the knowledge of our beginnings could indeed have originated with the forefathers of the Hindus, in which case the earlier origins of humankind could be more ancient still and possibly traceable back to those mysterious mountains, the Himalayas. Not forgetting that Lord Shiva's favoured residence was on Mount Kailasa (known also as the mythical Mount Meru) and often quoted as the 'navel of the world' as well as the 'site of the seven heavens' of the God Source ruled by Lord Brahma. It was here that Lord Shiva's consort Parvati is supposed to have resided with him when she became known as the 'daughter of the mountain'.

Throughout history much gets altered or re-written to suit the victors or the political climate over the passage of time, but when it comes to the ancient Hindus some of the oldest works are still in existence and these can give us the opportunity to delve deeper to find the greater truths within them, more so perhaps than in any other subject in the world.

Which was why I had sought to find the 'core' on all of humanity and marry it up with the knowledge given to us all on our own palm leaves which destiny had handed down, yet which had only now been revealed and shared.

I wondered. Perhaps it was just enough evidence to prove to myself at least that the written treatises and works were some of the most incredible and beneficial things that have ever been done to aid us all on our journey, and that the ancient Sanskrit writers were in fact spiritual initiates with a mission just like Saint Kausika and the six others. And the initiator of it all, bless him, would then be Lord Shiva.

In this case, what Lord Shiva called into creation at that beginning time will prove to have far greater significance than the Mayan Calendar (due to come to an end in December 2012), and will herald a time when the very consciousness of Mankind will begin to understand the real truth of our beginning.

CHAPTER ELEVEN

Taking Stock
Andrew's Verdict:

I was very greatly shocked and disturbed by all that I'd been told by the Naadi reader that day, and the manner in which it was given to me. It made no difference in the end how small, great or mind-blowing the extraordinary number of correct details there were. To this day, several years later, I still have the greatest trouble comprehending just how all that accurate information could have been arrived at, many elements of which I had completely forgotten or was unaware of, making their significance to me only the greater. And then, for me to have heard it all in a country thousands of miles away from my own, and from people with a wholly different culture and background who think and speak in an entirely different language, it all still beggars belief... particularly when they hadn't known that I even existed until the moment I crossed their doorway.

And yet, and yet... I'm intrigued to find that my questioning still continues today, even with the evidence that was given to me. I have never been one to readily accept that all we do and how we do it has already been fully mapped out, determined and set. To me it makes a mockery of any supposed free will if we merely run along rails that have been laid down beforehand, and I'd never been one to dwell on – let alone believe – that the sins or wrongs we do in one life will be carried over to the next, to hamper, hinder and blight our onward passage unless and until they are cleansed, purged and paid for.

Nice as such cosmic justice might be as a concept, I fancy it will miss most of us (willingly no doubt, and without too many backward glances) as it certainly did me until I was led, nervous and ashamed, into the *puja* room to begin making my amends. While there's a part of me that would happily have paid lip service to the penance that I undertook that day (just in case), after what I'd already heard I was not in any way prepared to risk it. So however implausible it sounds and however much I may continue to baulk intellectually at such concepts, emotionally I have been suitably chastened and brought to heel. The reality of 'sin' is very real to me now.

I have to confess that, so far, wherever I've looked or whatever I've heard or learnt since, I've found no other explanation as to how the Naadis manage to do all this other than the way they profess it to be – via Sri Kausika's palm leaf transcription of Lord Shiva's words all about my life, as copied and recopied over the centuries and left lying dormant until the precise time I was destined to meet up with it in New Delhi.

You can take it from me that it's a very strange feeling indeed to find out you have been expected and awaited by a palm leaf, one that is probably a few hundred years old, and then for that leaf to reveal all of your innermost secrets and actions. Not when you're someone like me, who normally ridicules and casually dismisses any such notions.

Yet I still wonder about it … how could the Naadis have known my parents' Christian names, about my stillborn brother or our failed intention to adopt a child? Or about my mother's sudden turn for the worse that very day, let alone my impending stomach operation which had given me no warning? No well-meaning friend could have known such intimate, private and personal details beforehand even if they had been knowledgeable enough and present to do so, which they weren't. And no eavesdropping spy could have overheard or picked up on any of them from the few mumbled conversations that Angela and I had had whilst waiting in the Naadis' reception, for none of these things would have even crossed our minds, let alone be mentioned there, or anywhere in Delhi. No one could have known of these things, or arranged it so that they would all come up correctly. Even Angela was totally unaware of several of the truths they told me.

So for all that I learnt that day (and have learnt since) about the Naadis and myself, I now find myself strangely no further forward at all in my quest to find out all about them, or to find any other way they could have found out all that they knew about me. Whatever questions I've raised or articles I have researched, read, tried to understand or even dismissed, somehow they have managed to remain as elusive as ever. And just as magical – every bit as much the 'hidden oracle' as when we first started.

Now, it could be that I've yet to stumble across the answer, that I've missed or failed to see what has been staring me in the face – it could indeed be so. But while I'm happy to concede that my enquiries and my research may have been limited for all manner of reasons, I still don't believe that I could have overlooked any obvious, glaring detail that could have alerted me to there being something else or some other way that they do it.

So while I've since seen and read other 'testimonies' on the web and elsewhere from people who have been to – and been disappointed by – the Naadis (but not ours I think) from the readings they have received, I can only respond that this was not how it was for me, as my own testimony makes abundantly clear. For me they could not have been more stunningly accurate about the whole of my life up to that very moment in time – and now beyond.

* * *

And I'm still left with the big question: can the Naadis truly access both the future and the past?

From my own experience I can only say it certainly feels so, however hare-brained and extraordinary it sounds, for I've found nothing yet to debunk it. Whatever my commonsense says, I firmly now believe that no cold-reading, lucky guesswork or skulduggery of the cleverest sort could have told me all of the detail found on 'my' leaf that day, meeting it as I did (so I thought) by sheer chance, but in fact reuniting at the only moment we ever could or would.

As the Naadis say, faith is the bedrock of their system and only those who have faith and are destined to find them will do so. Those who aren't destined to find them won't, they say, being most unlikely to discover that Naadi astrology even exists. So I recommend you have faith, even if like me it's still tempered with an amused and bemused skepticism afterwards. Emotionally I am undoubtedly all theirs now, even if intellectually I still like to carp and wriggle.

Bear in mind that you will be reading this book for a reason, even if you haven't yet realized it – your leaf will be summoning you whether you know it or not. So I wish you every success in your search. Believe me, it's an appointment you most surely do not want to miss.

And whatever you are then told, your reading, if true, will give you much pause for thought, for the Naadis say it is not enough to know whether your destiny is good or bad. You also have to have the opportunity to change it as you would like, to make amends, recognize and remove your sins to start afresh, setting your life back on course to achieve all that your soul has chosen and still wishes for.

I like that one – it's a great positive after all the negatives you have so unexpectedly had thrown at you. And while Angela may have trouble with the notion of changing your destiny from that which was written, after what I heard am I really one to say that the knowledge was not there already, or that it couldn't be changed if it is meant to be changed once I'd finished my *puja*? It is up to each of us in the end.

Perhaps you *can* change your future and have free will as well? Maybe all is not cast in stone, as hearing what your leaf tells you might first imply. Maybe all I was actually doing by visiting the Naadis and carrying out my *puja* was traveling down the road already laid for me. For my part, since returning from the Naadis and acting positively upon the 'remedies' they gave me, I am now much more relaxed, laid back and happier, and even more happy to go along with it. Given how much it disclosed and got right in both my present and my past, I'm really not going to start quibbling about any of what it foretold in my future.

And in believing and affirming that, of course, it will happen in just the way the Naadis said it will. Both my faith and my mind tell me that much at least. *Cogito ergo sum* goes the saying, but in my case it's simply a question of 'I am what I think'.

So I'm canceling the life policies.... Why continue paying them when I already know I'm living until my early eighties?

* * *

Angela's View:

I have fully embraced the Naadi experience.

Something happened when I first heard of them, when my friend spoke of them on the telephone just before we went to India for the first time in 2004. On reflection I must have had a sense of knowing, I suppose, rather like the feeling you get when you hear something that makes you sure deep down that there is a truth behind what is being said.

And it can't have been my friend's experience, as she had not even been to see them and knew only the sparsest of details about them at the time. But it changed as soon as she told me Deepak Chopra had been to them earlier that year, whose whole experience with them had apparently resonated very strongly with his life today. Of course, it certainly helps if someone famous, whom you respect, has personally underwritten their own experience with the mysterious palm leaf readers.

I somehow knew even then that Andrew would get his life reading, and was over the moon at the prospect. To me this was an incredible opportunity for him to hear the story of his life from complete strangers, and I had this driving force in me and a great sense of joy about it all. So how did I know then that it would be so? I can't tell you, except to say again that it was my own intuitive sense of knowing. Before we even left to take the trip I felt it was going to be the biggest catalyst in expanding Andrew's perception towards life and adding a spiritual dimension to his thinking.

On meeting the Naadis I hadn't given any of this much thought beforehand, but they certainly did have a great sense of calm about them.

I don't think this was simply because they didn't speak much if any English, it was more the reverence that permeated everywhere in, around and about them. They are happy and friendly, with a very uncommercial, laid-back attitude, and you cannot but admire their lack of stress and cool approach to everything. Most of us surely welcome and react well and warmly to that.

When I listened to Andrew's first session, when all the significant questions were asked to pinpoint his personal leaf, I felt very humbled by the experience. Yet inside I was brimming over with excitement that at any time he was going to hear his whole life unfold before him. And it might just be as I believed and had thought all along.

When my turn came, the next day, I was a little bemused. I love the adventure of life and I often get a feeling of excitement before an event, but this was different. I have never experienced a reading on my whole life, from birth to death, let alone in two-year tranches. Since childhood I had had a real sense of the significant areas of my life, including visions of specific happenings, and have received knowledge in advance of time on future events, through telepathic hearing or in visions. This has all been done as a medium and an intuitive. But trust me, it's not even remotely the same as sitting in a chair and hearing it read out to you step by step, the positive and the negative, both sides of the coin.

Nor is it a matter of absorbing the information, remembering only the best bits and cleverly forgetting the rest. You can't. It's all on the tape, and the strangest thing of all is that we all agree that every time we listen again to our tapes we hear more. The words never change, but their meaning does.

There were things said in my reading that could only have been me in my past, and when it came to the present (then 2004), it was exactly the situation I recognized. With regard to my life's work at that time, they said to me: "*what you are thinking of, and working on, at present will not happen... it is blocked, and not a good time*". Well, they were dead right there, and although I have this great determination and energy for everything I do it reminded me that I just had to relax, trust and go with the flow – all of which was something I really did need a mental jolt to do.

The reading went on to say when the 'good times' were and what would come about. As I am presently in that time period, watch this space – great things are happening. And just as importantly, the negative blocks that each and everyone suffers at sometime in life can be cleared by visiting the Naadis. To reach your full potential or optimum health potential, having washed away and purged your previous sins, who in their right minds would want to miss any such opportunities?

I don't follow any one religion and interestingly enough the Naadis did not care what religion I or anyone else that came to see them followed. While we had to go through *puja* ceremonies for our 'remedies', their ways never appeared in any way intrusive or wrong, and even seemed to add majesty and gravitas to the whole experience.

Yet what the Naadis are actually sharing is work that was given, taught and handed down eons ago, when humankind was supposed to be pretty rough and simple-minded. But it seems to me that that just isn't true – if anything, too many people in this day and age have lost the ability to think beyond the restrictive parameters of modern education and expected belief systems. I feel sure there was far more wisdom and knowledge held by the adept initiates back in those ancient times than most people today could realize.

Personally I feel the Naadi experience is one of the greatest benefits I could ever offer others, and to as many as possible – particularly those who are questioning their lives at present. And in this I can only speak through my own self-evidence and self-truth. If you have come this far you are drawn to have the experience, as Andrew and I were, and the way will be shown. You will quite naturally draw the opportunity in towards you. I am inclined to agree with the Naadis that there *is* a written time for you to go for your reading, so if you do decide to go – whether out of fascination, intrigue or because you have a healthy attitude – go and enjoy!

I will only add one piece of advice which stands for anything and everything you do or wish for in your life: never be attached to the outcome, whatever it is, release your wish for its time to come to you. Both Andrew and I have learnt to live our dream in the moment, ever since our leaves introduced us to our soul's purpose in this lifetime

CHAPTER TWELVE

A Guide to Planning Your Visit to the Naadi Readers

If after reading this you are drawn to visit the Naadi readers for your own palm leaf reading, we recommend in the strongest terms that you go there in person if it is at all possible, even if it means waiting for a year or two to afford the trip. It will give you time to plan a fantastic holiday, as well as a date with destiny, which would make the journey really worthwhile as well as change your life.

It is very difficult to get a Naadi reading unless you are there in person to make the request. Your enquiry may be ignored or put to the bottom of the list if you are not there in front of them, and the reading may not be authentic from some of the shop-front psychics that go under the broad banner of Naadi Astrologers across India unless you know they are reputable readers. Wherever you are in India, very few Indians, and certainly no Westerners, are up to speed on the genuine palm leaf readers. The best thing to remember if you are looking for the real thing, is that if they do not want your thumbprint then they are psychic astrologers, nothing more and nothing less.

Make sure you have access to a good interpreter too, one well used to nuances and subtleties of the several languages that can be used. At your request your hotel can arrange an interpreter and car with driver on a half-day basis – the cost is usually quite reasonable. Remember to ask for a Hindu/English speaker. They are all very respectful but they will try to assist you on as many trips as possible – it's all good business to them!

1) Taking the trip to India

India is such a vast and beautiful country, the regions vary so much. Whatever area you wish to visit, the people are friendly and helpful. When it comes to the hotels they range from expensive to very reasonable indeed, especially compared with the States or Europe. If you are booking your hotel when you book your flight, make sure they include meeting you at the airport in case you are arriving in the monsoon season. There is nothing worse than being soaked and feeling completely lost amongst hundreds of milling people all of whom are staring at you!

There is a varied cuisine covering everything western, Asian, Eastern, and of course exquisitely delicious spicy or temptingly mild curries, with many vegetarian dishes among the specialities. By following these two rules you may avoid 'Delhi-belly': do not drink the water unless it is bottled and unopened before you open it, and do not eat salads, ice-cream or take ice in your drinks.

A Reading in Delhi

You can book your first appointment either before you travel by phone (see Resources page) or go directly to the Naadi offices on your first day. You will be expected to put your thumbprint three times in the book with your first name, write whether you are male or female, and your hotel room and phone number. This will only take 10 minutes or so but the journey is likely to be at least half an hour wherever you decide to stay. On the third day onwards – it could take five days or even more – ask your hotel to phone the Naadi office on your behalf and find out if your leaf bundle has been found.

If so, get them to make an appointment for you as soon as possible, explaining that you are a visitor and only in the country for a short time. The Naadis are very kind and hospitable and will always make every effort to accommodate Westerners in advance of the locals.

When you have been found and you have an appointment.

You can have a full reading, like Andrew, which will consist of a life reading and a past life reading. This can take many hours. First they have to pinpoint your very own leaf, which alone can take hours. The sort of questions you will have to answer are listed below for guidance. They only want you to answer a simple 'Yes' or 'No' but the questions may search your past, so do not be tempted to bluff or it won't be your life they end up giving you.

A Reading in Chennai, Tamil Nadu, Southern India

Again you will have to book a flight to Delhi with a connecting flight to either Madurai or Coimbatore. Personally I think you would do better staying one night in Delhi and then flying on the next day. There are limits to how many hours of flying you can cope with and stay fresh and alert.

2) A friend goes on your behalf

If you ask a friend to take your details on your behalf, remember to give them a piece of paper with three copies of your thumbprints (right for a male and left for a female) plus all the salient points that are very personal to you from your very early life right up to date, because he or she will likely have to sit for several hours answering 'Yes' or 'No' to all the significant questions.

As examples:

Mother's first name: still alive   or dead & when:

Father's first name: still alive   or dead & when

Their backgrounds & careers, including marriages:

Number of brothers & sisters (including any who may have died in infancy):

Their ages:

Their background & careers:

Whether alive or dead and when and how:

Your own education and dates:

Your career and changes of career and when:

Where you live:

Your health:

Your temperament:

Your children or loss of, and dates of birth or ages and sex:
Your relationships:
Your marriages and when:
Good, bad or average:
Accidents, health issues or operations you have had:
What you are doing now:

When the Naadis have found your individual leaf, your friend will be expected to act as your surrogate and say 'Yes' or 'No' to all their questions.

When they have said 'Yes' to absolutely everything said on one leaf, you have been pinpointed fully. Then your surrogate will be expected to wait for up to an hour till the reading is ready, which will then be recorded on tape with your translator. The surrogate will also be respectfully asked to perform the rituals of *puja* on your behalf. The cost varies greatly but could be as much as $150 or more if you have some past misdeeds to repay. So make sure your friend has your mobile number and plenty of cash.

Please note: the Naadis only accept Rupees – no sterling, dollars, euros or credit cards. Rupees are not a valid currency outside India, so you have to spend them all while you're there or convert them back when you're leaving... or donate them to a good cause before you leave as part of your *puja*.

We wish you great luck on the journey of your lifetime.

RESOURCES

The Naadi practitioners that we visited and would recommend were:
Sri Kausika Mahasiva Naadi Jothilda Nilayam, E-1/209, Second Floor, Near Krishna Market, Lajpat Nagar-1, New Delhi 110024, tel. New Delhi 29817280 or 29813679. This Naadi centre is supervised by B. Raju, Naadi Astrologer.

Books:
India (Eyewitness Travel Guides) by DK Publishing

India – Culture Smart! A quick guide to customs and etiquette by Nicki Grihault

Footprint India (Footprint India Handbook) by Matt Barrett

O books
O is a symbol of the world, of oneness and unity. In different cultures it also means the "eye", symbolizing knowledge and insight, and in Old English it means "place of love or home". O books explores the many paths of understanding which different traditions have developed down the ages, particularly those today that express respect for the planet and all of life.

For more information on the full list of over 300 titles please visit our website
www.O-books.net

Back to the Truth
5,000 years of Advaita
Dennis Waite

A wonderful book. Encyclopedic in nature, and destined to become a classic. **James Braha**

    Absolutely brilliant...an ease of writing with a water-tight argument outlining the great universal truths. This book will become a modern classic. A milestone in the history of Advaita. **Paula Marvelly**

1905047614 500pp **£19.95 $29.95**

Beyond Photography
Encounters with orbs, angels and mysterious light forms
Katie Hall and John Pickering

The authors invite you to join them on a fascinating quest; a voyage of discovery into the nature of a phenomenon, manifestations of which are shown as being historical and global as well as contemporary and intently personal.

    At journey's end you may find yourself a believer, a doubter or simply an intrigued wonderer... Whatever the outcome, the process of journeying is likely prove provocative and stimulating and - as with the mysterious images fleetingly captured by the authors' cameras - inspiring and potentially enlightening. **Brian Sibley**, author and broadcaster.

1905047908 272pp 50 b/w photos +8pp colour insert **£12.99 $24.95**

Don't Get MAD Get Wise
Why no one ever makes you angry, ever!
Mike George

There is a journey we all need to make, from anger, to peace, to forgiveness. Anger always destroys, peace always restores, and forgiveness always heals. This explains the journey, the steps you can take to make it happen for you.
1905047827 160pp **£7.99 $14.95**

IF You Fall...
It's a new beginning
Karen Darke

Karen Darke's story is about the indomitability of spirit, from one of life's cruel vagaries of fortune to what is insight and inspiration. She has overcome the limitations of paralysis and discovered a life of challenge and adventure that many of us only dream about. It is all about the mind, the spirit and the desire that some of us find, but which all of us possess.
Joe Simpson, mountaineer and author of *Touching the Void*
1905047886 240pp **£9.99 $19.95**

Love, Healing and Happiness
Spiritual wisdom for a post-secular era
Larry Culliford

This will become a classic book on spirituality. It is immensely practical and grounded. It mirrors the author's compassion and lays the foundation for a higher understanding of human suffering and hope.
Reinhard Kowalski Consultant Clinical Psychologist
1905047916 304pp **£10.99 $19.95**

A Map to God
Awakening Spiritual Integrity
Susie Anthony

This describes an ancient hermetic pathway, representing a golden thread running through many traditions, which offers all we need to understand and do to actually become our best selves.
1846940443 260pp **£10.99 $21.95**

Punk Science
Inside the mind of God
Manjir Samanta-Laughton

Wow! Punk Science is an extraordinary journey from the microcosm of the atom to the macrocosm of the Universe and all stops in between. Manjir Samanta-Laughton's synthesis of cosmology and consciousness is sheer genius. It is elegant, simple and, as an added bonus, makes great reading.
Dr Bruce H. Lipton, author of *The Biology of Belief*
1905047932 320pp **£12.95 $22.95**

Rosslyn Revealed
A secret library in stone
Alan Butler

Rosslyn Revealed gets to the bottom of the mystery of the chapel featured in the Da Vinci Code. The results of a lifetime of careful research and study demonstrate that truth really is stranger than fiction; a library of philosophical ideas and mystery rites, that were heresy in their time, have been disguised in the extraordinarily elaborate stone carvings.
1905047924 260pp b/w + colour illustrations **£19.95 $29.95** cl

The 7 Ahas! of Highly Enlightened Souls
How to free yourself from ALL forms of stress
Mike George

7th printing

A very profound, self empowering book. Each page bursting with wisdom and insight. One you will need to read and reread over and over again! Paradigm Shift. I totally love this book, a wonderful nugget of inspiration.
PlanetStarz
1903816319 128pp 190/135mm **£5.99 $11.95**

God Calling
A Devotional Diary
A. J. Russell

46th printing

"When supply seems to have failed, you must know that it has not done so. But you must look around to see what you can give away. Give away something." One of the best-selling devotional books of all time, with over 6 million copies sold.
1905047428 280pp 135/95mm **£7.99** cl.
US rights sold

The Goddess, the Grail and the Lodge
The Da Vinci code and the real origins of religion
Alan Butler

5th printing

This book rings through with the integrity of sharing time-honoured revelations. As a historical detective, following a golden thread from the great Megalithic cultures, Alan Butler vividly presents a compelling picture of the fight for life of a great secret and one that we simply can't afford to ignore.

Lynn Picknett & **Clive Prince**
1903816696 360pp 230/152mm **£12.99 $19.95**

The Heart of Tantric Sex
A unique guide to love and sexual fulfilment
Diana Richardson

3rd printing
The art of keeping love fresh and new long after the honeymoon is over.
Tantra for modern Western lovers adapted in a practical, refreshing and
sympathetic way.
    One of the most revolutionary books on sexuality ever written. **Ruth**
Ostrow, News Ltd.
1903816378 256pp **£9.99 $14.95**

I Am With You
The best-selling modern inspirational classic
John Woolley

14th printing hardback
Will bring peace and consolation to all who read it. **Cardinal Cormac**
Murphy-O'Connor
0853053413 280pp 150x100mm **£9.99** cl
4th printing paperback
1903816998 280pp 150/100mm **£6.99 $12.95**

In the Light of Meditation
The art and practice of meditation in 10 lessons
Mike George

2nd printing
A classy book. A gentle yet satisfying pace and is beautifully illustrated.

Complete with a CD or guided meditation commentaries, this is a true gem among meditation guides. **Brainwave**

In-depth approach, accessible and clearly written, a convincing map of the overall territory and a practical path for the journey. **The Light**
1903816610 224pp 235/165mm full colour throughout +CD **£11.99 $19.95**

The Instant Astrologer
A revolutionary new book and software package for the astrological seeker
Lyn Birkbeck

2nd printing
The brilliant Lyn Birkbeck's new book and CD package, The Instant Astrologer, combines modern technology and the wisdom of the ancients, creating an invitation to enlightenment for the masses, just when we need it most! Astrologer **Jenny Lynch**, Host of NYC's StarPower Astrology Television Show
1903816491 628pp full colour throughout with CD ROM 240/180
£39 $69 cl

Is There An Afterlife?
A comprehensive overview of the evidence, from east and west
David Fontana

2nd printing
An extensive, authoritative and detailed survey of the best of the evidence supporting survival after death. It will surely become a classic not only of parapsychology literature in general but also of survival literature in particular. **Universalist**
1903816904 496pp 230/153mm **£14.99 $24.95**

The Reiki Sourcebook

Bronwen and Frans Stiene

5th printing

It captures everything a Reiki practitioner will ever need to know about the ancient art. This book is hailed by most Reiki professionals as the best guide to Reiki. For an average reader, it's also highly enjoyable and a good way to learn to understand Buddhism, therapy and healing. **Michelle Bakar**, Beauty magazine
1903816556 384pp **£12.99 $19.95**

Soul Power
The transformation that happens when you know
Nikki de Carteret

4th printing

One of the finest books in its genre today. Using scenes from her own life and growth, Nikki de Carteret weaves wisdom about soul growth and the power of love and transcendent wisdom gleaned from the writings of the mystics. This is a book that I will read gain and again as a reference for my own soul growth. **Barnes and Noble review**
190381636X 240pp **£9.99 $15.95**

1000 World Prayers
Marcus Braybrooke

This book is the most comprehensive selection of prayers from different traditions currently available. It is divided into five major sections: God (including silence, love, forgiveness), times and seasons, the changing scenes of life, the world and society, and the natural world. There is a

contemporary as well as traditional flavour. **Scientific and Medical Network Review**
1903816173 360pp 230/153mm **£12.99 $19.95**

Meditation: the 13 Pathways to Happiness

Jim Ryan

This book shows you how to meditate step by step, in an easy-to-follow and friendly guide. Each chapter is clarified and embellished by a meditation that enables the reader to reflect on and experience what has been said. Stories and quotes bring home it's relevance for millions of people from ancient times to the present.Used as a course by thousands around the world, these words are now published for the first time.
190504772X 80pp **£9.99 $19.95**

Peace Prayers from the world's faiths

Roger Grainger

Here eight different religions join together in peace to pray for peace, personal and global, under the auspices of the interfaith organization, The Week of Prayer for World Peace. This is a very practical prayer book, earthed in the pain of being human. It consists of seven weeks of prayer, each of which contains eight "days" of prayers and intercessions on particular themes connected with the overall theme of "Peace on earth and goodwill towards mankind".
1905047665 144pp **£11.99 $21.95**

Beyond All Reasonable Doubt

Michael Meredith

Genuinely open, scientifically thorough and often colourfully poetic. Exuberant clarity, the enrichment will extend way beyond the time spent actually reading it. Reform

An overriding feature of the book is the humility and scrupulous care that the author brings to his writing...an invitation to make contact with the transcendent within ourselves so that we may know in a similar way.
Scientific and Medical Network Review
1903816130 176pp **£8.99**

Jenny's Universe
How I told my daughter about galaxies, stardust and life
Kenneth Pederson

A consummately rational discourse about the building blocks of existence and the meaning embedded within the design of the universe. The key strength of the work is that it is credible and powerfully convincing, and remarkably humane. Pedersen even offers a hopeful paradigm for human evolution pertinent to our day and age, not based on new-age dreams, but on our biological and cultural heritage in the design of things. **Fearless Reviews**
1903816351 224pp **£14.99 $18.95** cl

Mysticism and Science
A call to reconciliation
S. Abhayananda

A lucid and inspiring contribution to the great philosophical task of our age - the marriage of the perennial gnosis with modern science. **Timothy Freke** author of *The Jesus Mysteries*
184694032X 144pp **£9.99 $19.95**

The Science of Oneness
A world view for the twenty-first century
Malcolm Hollick

A comprehensive and multi-faceted guide to the emerging world view. Malcolm Hollick brilliantly guides the reader intellectually and intuitively through the varied terrains of the sciences, psychology, philosophy and religion and builds up a vibrant picture that amounts to a new vision of reality for the 21st century. A veritable tour de force. **David Lorimer**, Programme Director, Scientific and Medical Network
1905047711 464pp 230/153mm **£14.99 $29.95**

The Thoughtful Guide to Science and Religion
Using science, experience and religion to discover your own destiny
Michael Meredith

This is a rich book that weaves science, experience and religion together with significant experiences from the author's own life. It ranges widely through the sciences and different religious traditions. A gem for the modern spiritual seeker. **Scientific and Medical Network Review**
1905047169 208pp **£10.99 $19.95**

The Wave
A life-changing insight into the heart and mind of the cosmos
Jude Currivan

2nd printing
Rarely does a book as fine as The Wave come along - this is a true treasure trove of ancient and current learning, covering a wide variety of interests. Accessible, interesting, educational and inspiring. The reader will find that both the intellect and the heart are gratified with this book, and that on a deeper level, much of it feels right - and that may be the best kind of

knowledge. **Merlian News**
1905047339 320pp **£11.99 $19.95**

The 9 Dimensions of the Soul
Essence and the Enneagram
David Hey

The first book to relate the two, understanding the personality types of the Enneagram in relation to the Essence, shedding a new light on our personality, its origins and how it operates. Written in a beautifully simple, insightful and heartful way and transmits complex material in a way that is easy to read and understand. **Thomas O. Trobe**, Founder and Director of Learning Love Seminars, Inc.
1846940028 176pp **£10.99 $19.95**

Aim for the Stars...Reach the Moon
How to coach your life to spiritual and material success
Conor Patterson

A fascinating, intelligent, and beneficial tool and method of programming your mind for success. The techniques are fast to achieve, motivating, and inspiring. I highly recommend this book. **Uri Geller**
1905047274 208pp **£11.99 $19.95**

Amulets
Kim Farnell

This is a wonderful book for those interested in learning about amulets and how to create them. Farnell's expertise makes her the ideal guide. Her knowledge is sound and her instructions are always clear and easy to follow. The strength of this book lies in it being one of easy access and also very well presented in its structure and internal logic. It makes an ideal reference book for anyone of a serious interest, being equally suited to beginners and experts alike. **Deborah Houlding**, author of *The Houses: Temples of the Sky*

1846940060 160pp **£9.99 $14.95**

Developing Spiritual Intelligence
The power of you
Altazar Rossiter

This beautifully clear and fascinating book is an incredibly simple guide to that which so many of us search for. **Dr Dina Glouberman**

1905047649 240pp **£12.99 $19.95**

Happiness in 10 Minutes
Brian Mountford

Brian Mountford-in exploring "happiness"-celebrates the paradox of losing and finding at its heart. At once both profound and simple, the book teaches us that to be fully alive is to be in communion and that gratitude leads us into the mystery of giving ourselves away-the path of true joy. **Alan Jones**, Dean of Grace Cathedral, San Francisco, author of *Reimagining Christianity.*

1905047770 112pp b/w illustrations **£6.99 $9.95**

Head Versus Heart-and our Gut Reactions
The 21st century enneagram
Michael Hampson

A seminal work, whose impact will continue to reverberate throughout the 21st century. Brings illumination and allows insights to tumble out. **Fr Alexander**, Worth Abbey

Printed and bound by CPI Group (UK) Ltd, Croydon, CR0 4YY

19038169000 320pp **£11.99 $16.95**